LIFE AMONG THE SAVAGES

By Shirley Jackson

THE ROAD THROUGH THE WALL

THE LOTTERY

HANGSAMAN

LIFE AMONG THE SAVAGES

LIFE AMONG THE SAVAGES

by Shirley Jackson

ACADEMY
CHICAGO

Published in 1990 by
Academy Chicago Publishers
213 West Institute Place
Chicago, Illinois 60610

Portions of this book have appeared in other forms
in *Charm, Collier's, Good Housekeeping, Harper's,*
Mademoiselle, Woman's Day, Woman's Home Companion.
The section which was originally published as
"Charles" in *Mademoiselle* and *The Lottery* is included
here at the particular request of my older son.

Published by arrangement with Farrar, Straus & Giroux, Inc.

Printed and bound in the USA.

Library of Congress Cataloging-in-Publication Data

Jackson, Shirley, 1919-1965.
Life among the savages.

1. Jackson, Shirley, 1919-1965—Biography.
2. Authors, American—20th century—Biography.
I. Title
PS3519.A392Z465 1989 818'.5409 [B] 89-18257
ISBN 0-89733-342-X

For the Children's Grandparents

LIFE AMONG THE SAVAGES

ONE

OUR HOUSE IS old, and noisy, and full. When we moved into it we had two children and about five thousand books; I expect that when we finally overflow and move out again we will have perhaps twenty children and easily half a million books; we also own assorted beds and tables and chairs and rocking horses and lamps and doll dresses and ship models and paint brushes and literally thousands of socks. This is the way of life my husband and I have fallen into, inadvertently, as though we had fallen into a well and decided that since there was no way out we might as well stay there and set up a chair and a desk and a light of some kind; even though this *is* our way of life, and the only one we know, it is occasionally bewildering, and perhaps even inexplicable to the sort of person who does not have that swift, accurate conviction that he is going to step on a broken celluloid doll in the dark. I cannot think of a preferable way of life, except one without children and without books, going on soundlessly in an apartment hotel where they do the cleaning for you and send up your meals and all you have to do is lie on a couch and—as I say, I cannot think of a preferable way of life, but then I have had to make a good many compromises, all told.

I look around sometimes at the paraphernalia of our living—sandwich bags, typewriters, little wheels off things—and marvel at the complexities of civilization with which we surround ourselves; would we be pleased, I wonder, at a wholesale elimination of these things, so that we were reduced only to necessities (coffeepot, typewriters, the essential little wheels off things) and then—this happening usually in the springtime—I begin throwing things away, and it turns out that although we can live agreeably without the little wheels off things, new little wheels turn up almost immediately. This is, I suspect, progress. They can make new little wheels, if not faster than they can fall off things, at least faster than I can throw them away.

I remember the morning, long ago, when the landlord called. Our son Laurie was three and a half, and our daughter Jannie was six months old, and I had the lunch almost ready and the diapers washed, along with the little shirts and the nightgowns and the soakers and the cotton blankets, and they were all drying on the line (and I don't care what *any*one says, that's a morning's work, when you consider that I had also made brownies and emptied the ashtrays) and then the landlord called. He was a kindly man, and a paternal one, so that he asked first about my health, and my husband's health, and then he asked how was our boy? and how was the baby? and when I said that we were all fine, fine, he said that of course we were aware that our lease was up? I said well, no, we hadn't really known that our lease was up. So he said well, he supposed that we hadn't looked at the lease recently and I (wondering if that was the paper Laurie had torn up and eaten) said that it had been quite a while, really, since we sat down together and read over our lease. That was too bad, he said. Wasn't it, I said. Because, he said, his voice gentle, the apartment had been rented to someone else. After a minute I said rented? to someone *else?* Then I laughed and said what were *we* supposed to do—move? He said well, yes, we were supposed to do just that.

"Naturally," he went on, "we could evict you if we wanted to."

"You could?" I was thinking of letters to the president, appeals for the sake of our two small children. "We'd much rather you'd just move out," he said.

"But where?"

He laughed genially. "Ask me another," he said. "Apartments are mighty tough to find these days."

"I suppose we could take a look around," I said dubiously. Letters, I was thinking, sue them for the piece of plaster that fell on my husband while he was shaving: lawyers.

"We'll expect to take possession around May first," he said.

"Today is March twenty-fifth," I said.

"That's right," he said. "Rent almost due," and he laughed again.

The next day we got a letter saying that it was "first notice of warning to evict." I began to think in terms of pouring boiling oil from the windows and barricading the doors with the dining room table. What made both of us even angrier was the fact that we had never had any intention of renewing our lease, but had planned vaguely on moving as soon as we found another place. "The very idea," I told my husband indignantly, "renting this apartment to someone else without fixing that broken step. The one on the stairs."

"Leave a note for the new people about the cockroaches," my husband advised. He also advised strenuously against bringing suit for some undetermined reason (the piece of plaster? the neighbor's radio?) and said, patting me on the shoulder, that he knew how anxious I had been to find another place.

Our fondest dream had been to move to Vermont, to a town where a couple we knew had settled and from which they had written us glowing accounts of mountains, and children playing in their own gardens, and clean snow, and homegrown carrots, and now suddenly it looked overwhelmingly as though we moved either to Vermont or to a tent in the park. I called half a dozen city agents, and they all laughed as gaily as our landlord had laughed; "Got any relatives you could move in with?" one of them asked me.

Finally, two hardy adventurers making for unexplored territory, we left the children with their grandparents, got ourselves and our suitcases and our overshoes onto a train at the station, and set out, an advance scouting party, for the small town where our friends lived, and where the mountains were so high and the snow so clean. There was no doubt, we discovered, about the snow. Our city overshoes went in over their heads as we stepped off the train, and for the three days we were there we both went constantly with damp feet and small bits of ice melting against our socks.

One nice thing was, there were lots and lots of houses available. We heard this from a lady named Mrs. Black, a motherly old body who lived in a nearby large town, but who knew, as she herself pointed out, every house and every family in the state. She took us to visit a house which she called the Bassington house, and which would have been perfect for us and our books and our children, if there had been any plumbing.

"Wouldn't take much to put *in* plumbing," Mrs. Black told us. "Put in plumbing, you got a real nice house there."

My husband shifted nervously in the snow. "You see," he said, "that brings up the question of . . . well . . . money."

Mrs. Black shrugged. "How much would *plumbing* cost?" she demanded. "You put in maybe twelve, fifteen hundred dollars, you got a real nice house."

"Now look, if we had fifteen hundred dollars we could give an apartment superintendent—" my husband began, but I cut in quickly, "You must remember, Mrs. Black, that we want to *rent*."

"Rent, did you?" said Mrs. Black, as though this proved at last that we were mere fly-by-nights, lookers at houses for the pleasure of it. "Well, if *I* was you folks, small children and all, well, *I*'d buy."

"But money—" my husband said.

"Money?" said Mrs. Black scornfully. "Two, three thousand dollars." She thought. "On the other hand," she said brightly, "if you was to fix it up *yourselves*—set in the plumbing, do a little painting, fix a few things maybe, you might cut your price down considerable."

She was looking directly at my husband as she said this, and he smiled weakly and nodded, obviously for that brief moment taken in by the notion that he might himself set in the plumbing. "You got to *figure*," Mrs. Black pursued, "you put down maybe two, three thousand dollars, you get a first mortgage from Henry Andrews down to the bank, you sign to put in a few improvements—all you got to figure *there* is title, I think, and maybe equity, Henry Andrews can tell you just exactly *what*. Taxes, o'course. Insurance, you'd want, and then you figure heat and electric, and maybe you could get Bill Adams to put in the plumbing for you for less on account it's his wife's sister owns the house, and there you are. Ten, fifteen years, you got a real nice house here, and you *own* it. Other way, you'd still be paying rent."

"But money—" my husband said.

Mrs. Black continued smoothly, "Other hand," she said, "you might like the McCaffery house. Now *there's* one with plumbing."

The McCaffery house may have had plumbing for all we ever knew; we could not get to it because the dirt road leading up to the top of the hill where the house sat was impassable with snow. "Have to clear *this* out some," Mrs. Black said, as we all stood at the bottom of the hill looking up at the house.

A Mr. Miller, who wore a leather jacket and a cap with earmuffs, took us to see the Donald house. This was a pretty place, set in an acre of marsh, but we unreasonably required a furnace, which Mr. Miller figured we ought to be able to put in for maybe two, three thousand. "Heat it with stoves, *I* would," he said. "Don't cost's much to run's a furnace."

"Money—" my husband said.

"Might be," Mr. Miller said, looking doubtfully at my husband, "might be you're handy-like around a house?"

Mr. Faber, who wore checked hunting pants and rolled his own cigarettes, showed us the Grant house, which had only three rooms and a lovely garden, and the Exeter house, which was big and rambling and heated and even had plumbing. "Real nice house here," Mr. Faber said as we stood, wondering, in the panelled dining room. "Priced at fifty thousand, but he ought to come down some on *that*."

"Fif–" said my husband.

"Well," Mr. Faber said sadly, "I didn't suppose you cared to go *that* high, but I figured you'd enjoy *seeing* it."

Mrs. Black, who picked us up again at nine the next morning, took us to see the Hubbard house, which had been made over from an old farmhouse, and had lovely floors and high ceilings and fireplaces and clean colored walls and even a garage, but no bedrooms. "The living room *alone* is seventy foot," Mrs. Black said. "Studio type house, you might say." She hesitated. "Matter of three, four thousand to build on a wing," she suggested hopefully.

"But we want to *rent*," I said, wailing. "We don't want to put things in and build things on and plough things out, we want to rent a house that's all put together *before* we move in."

Mrs. Black sighed. "There's a nice place, the Exeter house," she said at last. "Real big, suit you folks fine. Priced at–"

By the end of the second day we had even looked at a barn which someone had thought he might just rent out, but there were two cows and a tractor in that, and even Mrs. Black's optimistic suggestion that we could easily make up the stalls into bedrooms for the children could not encourage us.

"Well," Mrs. Black said as she said goodbye to us in

front of our friends' house, "I guess you folks are pretty lucky you got a place to live in the city."

Wearily, that evening, we sat in the comfortable living room of our friends' house, sheltered beneath a roof, securely, though temporarily, housed, and tried frantically to plan. It was April second, we had had our second notice of warning to evict, and we had begun to think wildly of renting a trailer, or having the children live with their grandparents, or borrowing a tent and a canoe and exploring the Great Lakes.

"Exeter," my husband said, miserably, "Exeter, McCaffery, Grant. Bassington, Hubbard, Donald. McCaffery, Bassington, Donald, Grant. Exeter, Hubbard–"

"We just can't *live* in a house without plumbing," I said.

"Or a furnace," my husband said. "McCaffery, Hubbard–"

"Maybe we *could* get an extension from our landlord," I said without hope. "Maybe if he knew how hard we tried he might let us have a few weeks more."

Our friends sat, shaking their heads sympathetically, although their own home was paid for and firmly fixed upon its foundations, with its furnace working smoothly and its plumbing in repair.

"If we only had some *money*," my husband said and everyone sighed.

We had to take the train home the next day, and on the way to the station I stopped in at the one grocery in town for cigarettes. After I had paid him the grocer said, "Couldn't find a place, I guess."

"No," I said, surprised, although I was to learn later that the grocer not only knew our housing problems, but the ages and names of our children, the meat we had been served for dinner the night before, and my husband's income.

"To bad you weren't interested in the Fielding place," the grocer said.

"We didn't even hear about it," I said.

"Would have called you," the grocer said, "but Mae Black, *she* said you only wanted to buy. Not for sale, the Fielding house."

"What's it like?"

The grocer waved his hand vaguely. "Old," he said. "Been in the family a long time." He accepted a nickel from a small boy, helped him take the wrapper off a popsicle, and said, "Whyn't you call old Sam Fielding? I bet he'd be real glad to take you over there."

There was only one train a day from the town. If we stopped long enough to look at the Fielding house we would not be able to leave until tomorrow; I hesitated, and the grocer said, "Won't do any harm to *look*, anyway."

I went outside and put my head in through the window of the car where my husband was waiting with our host and hostess. "Ever hear of a house called the Fielding house?" I asked.

"The *Fielding* house?" said our hostess, and our host said, "What on earth do you want with *that?*"

"What's the matter with it?" I asked.

"Well," said our hostess, "it's a thousand years old, I think."

"A million," said our host. "It's . . ." He gestured helplessly. "It's got these big white pillars across the front," he said.

"Is there a house in back of the pillars?" my husband asked. "Because if there is, and it has plumbing and a furnace and bedrooms and they'll rent it to us, we're going to be living there."

The Fielding house was a very old house about a mile out of town. It was the oldest in its neighborhood and the third oldest in the township; we had passed it, we realized with something of a shock, several times when we drove with Mrs. Black or Mr. Miller or Mr. Faber to look at other houses. It had been built—I looked it up in the town history shortly after we moved in, when I was vainly trying to come to terms with it—about eighteen-twenty, by a doctor named Ogilvie, who set it up as a manor house in the center of a great farm. The classical revival was upon the county then, and Doctor Ogilvie modeled his house after, presumably, a minor Greek temple; he set up the four massive white pillars across the front, threw wings out to both sides and then, with true New England economy, left the house only one room deep behind its impressive facade. When the Ogilvie family died off or moved away, as it did shortly after the house was built, it passed into the hands of a family named Cortland, who sold off most of the farm land and changed Doctor Ogilvie's woodshed into a summer kitchen. The Cortlands eventually sold the house to a family named Fielding, who promptly bought back all the surrounding land, now somewhat built up with houses, rented the houses out, set up a lumber mill on the river that used to run across Doctor Ogilvie's farm, and hired their tenants as employees. It seemed from the town records that the original Fielding had been a farm hand for Doctor Ogilvie, and the family no doubt had their eyes on the place even then. As the town developed the Fieldings became wealthier, and eventually the final generation of authentic Fieldings died off in the house and the entire property went to three cousins, all of whom lived in severely modern houses in neighboring towns, doing handsomely on their interests in the lumber mill.

When the manor house was put up for rent it was as though a vital part of the town had slid imperceptibly into the river, and a great coolness arose between the Fielding heirs and the Bartletts, who owned the second oldest house in town. During the worst housing shortages, when the lumber mill was going full blast night and day, the old manor house on top of the hill stayed empty, its white pillars sagging and its driveway choked with dead leaves or smooth with unmarked snow. When we saw it first it looked faintly ridiculous, and even the fences on either side and along the front leaned a little bit away from it, without actually renouncing it, as though they deplored it privately and yet wanted to present a unified front to the world of inhabitants. Sam Fielding was the only one of the Fielding cousins who retained the family name and so it had apparently been felt that he was the logical one to show us the house; he was a small quiet old man with the slow voice of the thoughtful Vermonter, and he stood with us at the foot of the lawn and he and my husband and I stared silently up at the huge pillars, the spread wings, the iron weather vane which stared mutely back at us.

"That's it," said Mr. Fielding undeniably. "I'd like to get *some* use out of it." He looked away quickly, as though avoiding an accusing glance from the house. "Good house," he added.

"It looks so . . ." I hesitated. "Imposing," I said finally.

"Imposing," Mr. Fielding agreed. He declined a cigarette from my husband and took out a cigarette of his own; it was the same brand, but it was his own. "Clean it up some," he said, nodding his head at the house.

"May we go inside?" I asked. "If we *were* interested in the house, I'd rather like to see the inside."

"Door's open," Mr. Fielding said.

We hesitated, my husband and I. Mr. Fielding settled himself comfortably on a tree stump and crossed his legs. "Door's open," he said again.

Together my husband and I made our way to the front door, avoiding just in time the broken step that led onto the porch. Once among the pillars the sense of the house came upon one with a rush; here was a *house*, as compared with the makeshift McCafferies and Exeters. My husband tried the front door tentatively, and it swung open. Gingerly, watching out for broken floorboards, we went inside, into a wide hall shadowed by the pillars and backed by a straight, lovely, colonial stairway; somewhere to our right were a carpet flooded with red cabbage roses and a harmonium, under dark old pictures which seemed to lean forward a little to watch us, surprised; we went into a kitchen where a monumental ironwork stove threatened to fall on us, and in the kitchen there was a table thick with dust and on it were a dusty cup and a plate with two solid, ancient doughnuts on it. There was a chair pushed a little away from the table.

"I'm sorry we stayed," I said to my husband earnestly, my hands shaking as I looked at the two hideous doughnuts, "we interrupted their lunch, let's leave right away."

"If it weren't the only house in town . . ." he said, but he followed me rapidly outside.

Mr. Fielding rose to meet us as we came back down between the pillars, and when we were near him he said, "Weather's closing in. Snow before morning." He escorted us solemnly to the station, discussing the weather, and as our train came in he remarked, "Fix her up some, then, before you folks come in the spring."

"Tell me," I said, "how long since anyone's been *in* that house?"

"Not since the old man died," he said. "Four year I figure that might be."

"But to straighten it up?" I insisted. "Look over his things, or anything?"

"Never really figured it would rent," he said thoughtfully. "No sense rushing things."

He waved to us kindly when we got onto the train. During most of that next two weeks I held firmly to the impractical conviction that I didn't *care* if it was the last house in the town, or in the world for that matter, and I didn't *care* if it meant living in the park, I was not going to live in a house with two petrified doughnuts. The following week, however, we received a letter from Mr. Fielding, saying that the house was being fixed up, and did we feel that fifty dollars a month was too much rent?

"You seem to have taken the house," I said unjustly to my husband.

"It's probably because we went inside," he said. "No one else has ever gone inside, and that probably constitutes a lease."

A week later we received another letter from Mr. Fielding, saying that the house was all ready for us, except for the outside, which would be painted when the weather opened up. Since we had not answered his last letter, he figured that his rent was too high, and did we think we could manage forty?

A strong sense of guilt impelled my husband to write

back immediately saying that fifty dollars a month was fine; "before he *gives* it to us," he told me.

"But I'm not—" I said, realizing that of course I was.

I came up on the train, a day after my husband. I brought with me a wildly excited Laurie, and Jannie, in a basket; and all the way up on the train, crushed in between Laurie and the baby's basket and the suitcases and the sandwiches, I was wondering if anyone had thought to take away the kitchen table and the doughnuts: my husband had promised that if we really couldn't stand it we could try once more to find something in the city. Mr. Fielding was with my husband to meet us at the station, and when I saw Mr. Fielding again the whole clear sense of the house came back to me and I was ready to turn around and go back right then. He smiled at me cheerfully, said, "Afternoon, young fellow," to Laurie, and stared gravely at the baby for a minute; she stared back at him, and then he nodded to me and said reassuringly, "Fixed her up some."

I knew what he meant when I saw the house. It had been literally scraped clean, down to the wood in the walls. Mr. Fielding had put on new wallpaper, rich with great gorgeous patterns, the windows had been washed, the pillars straightened, the broken step repaired, and a cheerful man in the kitchen was putting the last touches of glittering white paint to the new shelving; there was a brand new electric stove and a new refrigerator, the floors had been repaired and varnished, a hornets' nest had been removed from the farthest pillar on the right. The lawn was just beginning to show green, and Laurie ran in and out between the pillars, touching every one, and then, shouting, up and down the straight stairway. In her basket Jannie smiled, looking up at the sky over the trees.

"It's beautiful," I said to Mr. Fielding, almost in tears. "I thought it would look like it did before."

"Needed some work done," Mr. Fielding agreed. Then he nodded at the new kitchen stove and said, "Did the old place good."

Just then our moving van arrived, and the three muscular, brazen fellows who had looked so natural carrying our furniture out of the apartment became abruptly incongruous carrying our small chairs and tables in between the pillars.

"Put in some more plumbing, too," Mr. Fielding said, and departed.

For the first week or so things were completely at cross-purposes. Our furniture, which had been more than adequate for a city apartment, here spread all too thinly among the echoing rooms of the house, and we had to fill out with odd tables and chairs brought from Mr. Fielding and from nearby second-hand shops. The house had grown enormously, I later learned, from Doctor Ogilvie's original structure. The Cortlands had added the summer kitchen, but the Fieldings had added on and on, so that the room which had been the summer kitchen, for instance, and hitched on to the back of the house in the first place, was now smack in the middle, tucked in among larger and sturdier rooms, and was no longer a kitchen at all but only a dark little room which was sometimes difficult to find. We had only three beds and we had six bedrooms, so Mr. Fielding sold us, for fifty cents, a bed that had been only recently taken out of the house and put into one of the capacious barns. We tried to buy the harmonium but the Fieldings had sold it to an antique dealer; we did buy the carpet with the cabbage roses, since it was the only one which would fit into the vast desert of the parlor; we declined, with one voice, the old kitchen table. All these things, the ones that had been in the house before, and other things which had been in similar old houses and knew their ways, fell naturally into good positions in the rooms, as though snatching the best places before the city furniture could crowd in. No matter how much we wanted to set our overstuffed chairs on either side of the living room fireplace, an old wooden rocker that Mr. Fielding had given us insisted upon pre-empting the center of the hearth rug and could not in human kindness be shifted. An old highboy, which was a contemporary of the rocker although it had come from a barn across town, took over the living room corner near the rocker, and the two of them lived there in silent companionship.

After a few vain attempts at imposing our own angular order on things with a consequent out-of-jointness and shrieking disharmony that set our teeth on edge, we gave in to the old furniture and let things settle where they would. An irritation persisted in one particular spot in the dining room, a spot which would hold neither table nor buffet and developed an alarming sag in the floor when I tried to put a radio there, until I found completely by accident that this place was used to a desk and would not be comfortable until I went out and found a spindly old writing table and set a brass inkwell on it.

There was a door to an attic that preferred to stay latched and would latch itself no matter who was inside; there was another door which hung by custom slightly ajar, although it would close goodhumoredly for a time when some special reason required it. We had five attics, we discovered, built into and upon and next to one another; one of them kept bats and we shut that one up completely; another, light and cheerful in spite of its one small window, liked to be a place of traffic and became, without any decision of ours, a place to store things temporarily, things that were moved regularly, like sleds and snow shovels and garden rakes and hammocks. The basement had an old clothesline hung across it, and after the line I put up in the back yard had fallen down for the third time I resigned myself and put up a new line in the basement, and clothes dried there quickly and freshly. We stocked the woodshed, since we had four fireplaces, and my husband discovered an odd pleasure in splitting wood, and the sound of an axe in the woodshed echoed agreeably through the kitchen. One bedroom chose the children, because it was large and light and showed unmistakable height-marks on one wall and seemed to mind not at all when crayon marks appeared on the wallpaper and paint got spilled on the floor. We put bookcases in the little dark room downstairs, and after the second week my husband got so he could find it nine times out of ten.

It *was* a good old house, after all. Our cats slept on the rocking chair; our friends came to call. We accustomed ourselves to trading at certain stores and we bought our cheese locally and we found a doctor and a dog; Laurie entered the community nursery school and learned, as I had, to identify the house by saying "It's the old Fielding house—the one with the pillars." Toward the end of our first year there the painter arrived to do the outside of the house, and he painted it white with green trim, the colors it had always been painted before; indeed, I doubt if he owned any other colors of paint. "Not many houses like *this* nowadays," he told me, smiling benignly down at me from the top of his ladder, "don't find houses *built* like this any more."

I looked from the front porch in through the glass of the front door, seeing the slim line of the stairway and the bright curtains in the dining room. "It's a good old house," I said.

"Can always tell by the cats," the painter said enigmatically.

I found that, where in the city I had always been too busy to do anything at all, I was now making odd things like gingerbread and cabbage salad. Laurie started a crude garden out back, and Jannie took her first step in the dining room. Once I left both of them with our next-door neighbor, and went into the city for a wild two-day shopping trip; when I wandered into our old neighborhood and stood in front of our old apartment house I could only think how small and dirty it looked. "No pillars *there*," I told myself with deep gratification, and wished I could write our old landlord and tell *him*.

So, the house was old when we found it, and noisy when we entered it, and it took very little time for it to fill up. Our children brought in friends and rocking horses and paint brushes, we brought in friends and books and little wheels off things. I learned to make pie crust—although I have not the touch of a born pie-maker, I am afraid. People from the city began driving up for weekends in the nice weather.

Jannie spoke for a long time about a faraway voice in the house which sang to her at night, and we put the Christmas tree in the corner of the living room where the lights shone at night out between the pillars; we raked leaves on the front lawn and went sledding down the hillside. We began to speak slightingly of city-folk.

I have, as I say, never found a way of life preferable to this; its only fault—aside from the back-breaking labor and the vicious pie crusts which refuse to brown—is that it goes on and on, without, it seems, any major change at all. I observe my neighbors and it seems to me that they are content to live on, registering and employing each day but not in the least distinguishing one day beyond another, and, although that is obviously the best way of passing time, it makes, I feel, for little or no excitement. Even a major event (like our hurricane, or the time we had the flood, or that terribly heavy snow when all the electricity was out for three days) tends to become, by the next day, only a remembered landmark—"that was two days, I recollect, before the hurricane, because we had all those raspberries to set out . . ."—and even the last trump will, I am afraid, make no more of an impression on our community (". . . well, now, let's see; that there bugle blowed around about three in the afternoon, and I remember the day because it was the day I w's supposed to hammer on the boards on that there gate, and here it's been maybe six weeks since that ol' bugle, and there hangs the gate right now . . ."). When I think about it, I can only remember the year Laurie was born because I was waiting to get a new winter coat.

One of the most unnerving, and least original, observations I have made about my children is that as these years turn and Christmas inevitably follows the fourth of July and the fourth of July inevitably follows Christmas, they tend to grow older. Every October, for instance, Laurie has a birthday. Every November, incredible as it may sound, Jannie has a birthday; the fact that I also have a birthday every December is unfortunately entirely believable but somehow less heartwarming. When we first came to the house in the country, Laurie was something over three years old, and Jannie was six months, and then suddenly—although I had in the meantime grown a year older, and so had my husband, and we wished one another "Happy Birthday" very properly—Jannie was almost two and had become a legitimate member of the family named Jannie (instead of Baby, or The Baby), and Laurie was just short of five and was clamoring for the right to vote on domestic policies.

The day Laurie started kindergarten he renounced corduroy overalls with bibs and began wearing blue jeans with a belt; I watched him go off the first morning with the older girl next door, seeing clearly that an era of my life was ended, my sweet-voiced nursery-school tot replaced by a long-trousered, swaggering character who forgot to stop at the corner and wave goodbye to me.

He came home the same way, the front door slamming open, his cap on the floor, and the voice suddenly become raucous shouting, "Isn't anybody *here?*"

At lunch he spoke insolently to his father, spilled Jannie's milk, and remarked that his teacher said that we were not to take the name of the Lord in vain.

"How *was* school today?" I asked, elaborately casual.

"All right," he said.

"Did you learn anything?" his father asked.

Laurie regarded his father coldly. "I didn't learn nothing," he said.

"Anything," I said. "Didn't learn anything."

"The teacher spanked a boy, though," Laurie said, addressing his bread and butter. "For being fresh," he added with his mouth full.

"What did he do?" I asked. "Who was it?"

Laurie thought. "It was Charles," he said. "He was fresh. The teacher spanked him and made him stand in a corner. He was awfully fresh."

"What did he do?" I asked again, but Laurie slid off his chair, took a cookie, and left, while his father was still saying "See here, young man."

The next day Laurie remarked at lunch, as soon as he sat down, "Well, Charles was bad again today." He grinned enormously and said, "Today Charles hit the teacher."

"Good heavens," I said, mindful of the Lord's name, "I suppose he got spanked again?"

"He sure did," Laurie said. "Look up," he said to his father.

"What?" his father said, looking up.

"Look down," Laurie said. "Look at my thumb. Gee, you're dumb." He began to laugh insanely.

"Why did Charles hit the teacher?" I asked quickly.

"Because she tried to make him color with red crayons," Laurie said. "Charles wanted to color with green crayons so he hit the teacher and she spanked him and said nobody play with Charles but everybody did."

The third day—it was Wednesday of the first week—Charles bounced a seesaw onto the head of a little girl and made her bleed and the teacher made him stay inside all during recess. Thursday Charles had to stand in a corner during storytime because he kept pounding his feet on the floor. Friday Charles was deprived of blackboard privileges because he threw chalk.

On Saturday I remarked to my husband, "Do you think kindergarten is too unsettling for Laurie? All this toughness and bad grammar, and this Charles boy sounds like such a bad influence."

"It'll be all right," my husband said reassuringly. "Bound to be people like Charles in the world. Might as well meet them now as later."

On Monday Laurie came home late, full of news. "Charles," he shouted as he came up the hill; I was waiting anxiously on the front steps, "Charles," Laurie yelled all the way up the hill, "Charles was bad again."

"Come right in," I said, as soon as he came close enough. "Lunch is waiting."

"You know what Charles did?" he demanded, following me through the door. "Charles yelled so in school they sent a boy in from first grade to tell the teacher she had to make Charles keep quiet, and so Charles had to stay after school. And so all the children stayed to watch him."

"What did he do?" I asked.

"He just sat there," Laurie said, climbing into his chair at the table. "Hi Pop, y'old dust mop."

"Charles had to stay after school today," I told my husband. "Everyone stayed with him."

"What does this Charles look like?" my husband asked Laurie. "What's his other name?"

"He's bigger than me," Laurie said. "And he doesn't have any rubbers and he doesn't ever wear a jacket."

Monday night was the first Parent-Teachers meeting, and only the fact that Jannie had a cold kept me from going; I wanted passionately to meet Charles' mother. On Tuesday Laurie remarked suddenly, "Our teacher had a friend come see her in school today."

"Charles' mother?" my husband and I asked simultaneously.

"Naaah," Laurie said scornfully. "It was a man who came and made us do exercises. Look." He climbed down from his chair and squatted down and touched his toes. "Like this," he said. He got solemnly back into his chair and said, picking up his fork, "Charles didn't even *do* exercises."

"That's fine," I said heartily. "Didn't Charles want to do exercises?"

"Naaah," Laurie said. "Charles was so fresh to the teacher's friend he wasn't *let* do exercises."

"Fresh again?" I said.

"He kicked the teacher's friend," Laurie said. "The teacher's friend told Charles to touch his toes like I just did and Charles kicked him."

"What are they going to do about Charles, do you suppose?" Laurie's father asked him.

Laurie shrugged elaborately. "Throw him out of school, I guess," he said.

Wednesday and Thursday were routine; Charles yelled during story hour and hit a boy in the stomach and made him cry. On Friday Charles stayed after school again and so did all the other children.

With the third week of kindergarten Charles was an institution in our family; Jannie was being a Charles when she cried all afternoon; Laurie did a Charles when he filled his wagon full of mud and pulled it through the kitchen; even my husband, when he caught his elbow in the telephone cord and pulled telephone, ash tray, and a bowl of flowers off the table, said, after the first minute, "Looks like Charles."

During the third and fourth weeks there seemed to be a reformation in Charles; Laurie reported grimly at lunch on Thursday of the third week, "Charles was so good today the teacher gave him an apple."

"What?" I said, and my husband added warily, "You mean Charles?"

"Charles," Laurie said. "He gave the crayons around and he picked up the books afterward and the teacher said he was her helper."

"What happened?" I asked incredulously.

"He was her helper, that's all," Laurie said, and shrugged.

"Can this be true, about Charles?" I asked my husband that night. "Can something like this happen?"

"Wait and see," my husband said cynically. "When

you've got a Charles to deal with, this may mean he's only plotting."

He seemed to be wrong. For over a week Charles was the teacher's helper; each day he handed things out and he picked things up; no one had to stay after school.

"The P.-T.A. meeting's next week again," I told my husband one evening. "I'm going to find Charles' mother there."

"Ask her what happened to Charles," my husband said. "I'd like to know."

"I'd like to know myself," I said.

On Friday of that week things were back to normal. "You know what Charles did today?" Laurie demanded at the lunch table, in a voice slightly awed. "He told a little girl to say a word and she said it and the teacher washed her mouth out with soap and Charles laughed."

"What word?" his father asked unwisely, and Laurie said, "I'll have to whisper it to you, it's so bad." He got down off his chair and went around to his father. His father bent his head down and Laurie whispered joyfully. His father's eyes widened.

"Did Charles tell the little girl to say *that?*" he asked respectfully.

"She said it *twice*," Laurie said. "Charles told her to say it *twice*."

"What happened to Charles?" my husband asked.

"Nothing," Laurie said. "He was passing out the crayons."

Monday morning Charles abandoned the little girl and said the evil word himself three or four times, getting his mouth washed out with soap each time. He also threw chalk.

My husband came to the door with me that evening as I set out for the P.-T.A. meeting. "Invite her over for a cup of tea after the meeting," he said. "I want to get a look at her."

"If only she's there," I said prayerfully.

"She'll be there," my husband said. "I don't see how they could hold a P.-T.A. meeting without Charles' mother."

At the meeting I sat restlessly, scanning each comfortable matronly face, trying to determine which one hid the secret of Charles. None of them looked to me haggard enough. No one stood up in the meeting and apologized for the way her son had been acting. No one mentioned Charles.

After the meeting I identified and sought out Laurie's kindergarten teacher. She had a plate with a cup of tea and a piece of chocolate cake; I had a plate with a cup of tea and a piece of marshmallow cake. We maneuvered up to one another cautiously and smiled.

"I've been so anxious to meet you," I said. "I'm Laurie's mother."

"We're all so interested in Laurie," she said.

"Well, he certainly likes kindergarten," I said. "He talks about it all the time."

"We had a little trouble adjusting, the first week or so," she said primly, "but now he's a fine little helper. With lapses, of course."

"Laurie usually adjusts very quickly," I said. "I suppose this time it's Charles' influence."

"Charles?"

"Yes," I said, laughing, "you must have your hands full in that kindergarten, with Charles."

"Charles?" she said. "We don't have any Charles in the kindergarten."

It was soon after this meeting—the whole question of Charles having somehow dissipated and become without discussion a forbidden topic—that my husband, moved by some obscure impulse which may or may not have been connected with Charles, bought himself an air gun. I have never really believed that my husband is the Kit Carson type, but it is remotely possible that occasionally a feeling for the life romantic overcomes him; this air gun was large and menacing and he told me, in that terribly responsible voice men get to using when they are telling their wives about machinery, or guns, or politics, that he got it for target practice.

There had been a rat in the cellar, he said; he was sure he had seen a rat when he went down to start the furnace. So, of course, he was going to shoot it. Not trap it or poison it—that was for boys and terriers; *he* was going to shoot it.

For the better part of a Sunday morning he crouched dangerously at the open cellar door, waiting for the rat to show his whiskers, which the rat was kind enough not to do. Our two excellent cats were also staying inside, sitting complacently and with some professional interest directly behind my husband. The rat hunt was broken up when the kitchen door banged open and Laurie crashed in with three friends to see how his father shot the rat. Eventually, I suppose, the rat wandered off, although I do not see how he could conceivably have been frightened by the prospect of being shot. Probably he had never realized until then that he had strayed into a house with cats *and* children. At any rate, my husband and the cats, hunting in a pack, managed to bring down even better game; it must have been about the Tuesday after the rat hunt that our female cat, Ninki, who is something of a hunter, caught a chipmunk. She has done this before and will do it again, although I am sure she will never again ask my husband to sit in with her. The chipmunk she caught that morning—it was about nine-thirty—was not co-operative, and when Ninki brought him into the kitchen, where she usually brings chipmunks with some odd conviction that she must eat them in her own dish, the chipmunk ducked under her paw and raced madly to a rather tall plant on the window sill. The plant was just strong enough to bear the weight of one chipmunk, and Ninki, in a sort of frenzy, hurried into the dining room where my husband was just finishing his coffee and talked him into going into the kitchen to see her chipmunk in the plant. My husband took one look and went for his air gun.

Ninki was able to get onto the window sill, but the plant was tall enough and the pot it stood in shaky enough so that she could not quite reach the chipmunk, who was standing precariously on the very top of the plant. My husband drew a careful bead with the air gun and then found that unless he stepped up and held his weapon against the chipmunk's head, he stood a very good chance of missing the chipmunk, if not actually the cat, who was a large and intrusive target.

By this time, of course, I had put down my coffee cup and was standing in the doorway between the kitchen and the dining room, safely out of range as women should be when men are hunting, and saying things like "Dear, why don't you put a paper bag over it or something and take it outside?" and "Dear, don't you think it would be easier if—"

Ninki was by this time irritated beyond belief by the general air of incompetence exhibited in the kitchen, and she went into the living room and got Shax, who is extraordinarily lazy and never catches his own chipmunks, but who is, at least, a cat, and preferable, Ninki saw clearly, to a man with a gun. Shax sized up the situation with a cynical eye, gave my husband and his gun the coldest look I have ever seen a cat permit himself, and then leaped onto the window sill and sat on the other side of the flowerpot. It made a pretty little tableau: Ninki and Shax sitting on either side of the flowerpot and the chipmunk sitting on top of the plant.

After a minute the chipmunk—feeling rightly that all eyes were upon him—fidgeted nervously, and the plant began to sway. As the chipmunk was very nervous and the top of the plant very supple, soon the top of the plant began to swing from side to side, like a pendulum, so that the chipmunk, going faster and faster, rocked over to one cat and then to the other, grazing a nose of each, while they backed away dubiously. My husband still had his aim on the chipmunk, and *he* began to rock back and forth. When the cats finally realized what was happening, they took turns batting the chipmunk as he swung between them.

All of this happened so quickly that I believe—unless I prefer to move out I have no choice *but* to believe—that my husband pressed the trigger of the air gun without really meaning to, because it is certain that he missed the chipmunk and the cats, and hit the window. The crash sent cats, chipmunk, and Nimrod in all directions—the cats under the table, the chipmunk, with rare presence of mind, out the broken window, and my husband, with even rarer presence of mind, back to the dining room and to his seat at the table. I advanced from my post in the kitchen doorway and picked up the air gun from the floor; then, with what I regard as unique forbearance, I went for the broom and dustpan. All I permitted myself, spoken gently and without undue emphasis, was "Thank heaven Laurie is in school."

I was indulgent enough to return the air gun to my husband after a few days, but I would have thought that Ninki had more sense. Perhaps she never dreamed I would give the air gun back, or perhaps she just thought target practice around the house had been given up as impractical; perhaps, with some kind of feline optimism I cannot share, she believed that the chipmunk episode had been a freak, the sort of thing that might happen to any man confronting an oscillant chipmunk.

So it was not more than a week later that Ninki gave the air gun another chance. It was a cool evening, and I was lying on the couch with a blanket over me, reading a mystery story; my husband was sitting quietly in his chair reading the newspaper. We had just congratulated one another on the fact that it was now too late for casual guests to drop in, and my husband had mentioned three or four times that he thought he might like some of that pot roast in a sandwich before he went to bed. Then we heard Ninki's unmistakably triumphant mighty-hunter howl from the dining room.

"Look," I said apprehensively, "Ninki's got something, a mouse or something. *Make* her take it outside."

"She'll get it out by herself."

"But she'll chase it around and around and around the

dining room and kill it there and—" I gulped unhappily "—eat it. Get it out *now* while it's still alive."

"She won't—" my husband began, when Ninki's triumphant wail broke off with a muffled oath and Ninki herself came hurriedly to the dining room door and stared compellingly at my husband.

"Do you *always* need help?" he asked her crossly. "Seems to me a great big cat like you—"

I shrieked. Ninki lifted her head resignedly, as one whose bitterest views of fate have been confirmed; my husband gasped. Ninki's supper, a full-grown and horribly active bat, was sweeping magnificently down the length of the living room. For a minute I watched it with my mouth open and then, still yelling, buried my head under the blanket.

"My gun," I heard my husband shouting at Ninki, "where is my gun?"

Even under the blanket I could hear the flap of the bat's wings as it raced up and down the living room; I put my knees under my chin and my arms over my head and huddled under the blanket. Outside, they were stalking the bat; I could hear my husband tiptoeing warily down the room, with Ninki apparently right behind him, because he was saying, "Don't *hurry*, for heaven's sake, give me a chance to *aim*."

A hideous thought came to me. "Is it on me?" I said through my teeth, "just tell me once, is it on me, on the blanket? Ninki, *is* it? Is it?"

"Now you just stay perfectly still," my husband said reassuringly. "These things never stay in one place for very long. Why, only the other day I was reading in the paper about a woman who—"

"Is it on the *blanket?*" I insisted hysterically, "on *me?*"

"Listen," my husband said crossly, "if you keep on shaking like that, I'll *never* be able to hit it. Hold still, and I'm sure to miss you."

I do not know what the official world's record might be for getting out from under a blanket, flying across a room, opening a door and a screen door, and getting outside onto a porch with both doors closed behind you, but if it is more than about four seconds I broke it. I thought the bat was chasing me, for one thing. And I knew that, if the bat were chasing me, my husband was aiming that gun at it, wherever it was. Outside on the porch, I leaned my head against the middle pillar and breathed hard.

Inside, there was a series of crashes. I recognized the first as the report of the air gun. The second sounded irresistibly like a lamp going over, which is what it turned out to be. The third I could not identify from the porch, but my husband said later that it was Ninki trying to get out of the way of the air gun and knocking over the andirons. Then my husband spoke angrily to Ninki, and Ninki snarled. Each of them, it seemed, thought the other one had frightened the bat, which had left the blanket when I did, although not half so fast, and was now circling gaily around the chandelier.

"Come on in," my husband said through the door; he tried to open it but I was hanging on from the outside; "Come on in, it won't hurt you. I promise it won't."

"I'll stay out here," I said.

"It's just as frightened as you are," he said.

"It is *not*," I said.

Then he apparently spoke to Ninki again, because he said excitedly, "It's landing; keep away now, you'll be hurt."

There was a great noise of rushing and snarling and shooting, then a long silence. Finally I asked softly, "Are you all right?"

Another silence. "Are you all *right?*" I said.

Another silence. I opened the door a crack and peered in cautiously. My husband was sitting on the couch, beating his hands on his knees. The air gun was on the floor. Ninki and the bat were gone.

"Is it all right to come in?" I asked.

"I don't know," my husband said, looking at me bitterly, "have you got a ticket?"

"I mean," I said, "where's the bat?"

"She's taken it into the dining room," my husband said.

There was a nick in the wallpaper over the couch. In the dining room Ninki was growling pleasurably, deep in her throat. "She went faster than the pellet, is all," my husband said reasonably. "I was just getting ready to aim and she passed me and passed the pellet and hit the bat just as the pellet hit the wall."

"Hadn't you better get it out of the dining room?" I asked.

He began to beat his knees again. I went back to the couch, shook the blanket thoroughly to make sure there had been only one bat on it and that one was gone, and settled down in my chair with my mystery story. After a while Ninki came out of the dining room, nodded contemptuously at my husband, glanced at me and, with a grin at the air gun, got onto my husband's chair and went to sleep on his paper.

I took the air gun and put it on the top shelf of the pantry, where I believe it still is. Now and then it occurs to me that in case of burglars I can take it down to protect the house, but I really think one of the kitchen knives would be safer, if Ninki is not around to take care of me.

It was only the next morning that the man came to fix the glass in the kitchen window, and when Laurie, who was on his reluctant way to school, told the man his father had shot it out with a gun, I laughed cheerily and remarked that boys always had such good stories to cover their own misdeeds. Laurie looked at me in honest indignation, and I told him that he could take a package of gum from the pantry. Although I do not believe in actually encouraging children to tell lies, and do not in any case suppose that one pack of gum can cover up a flagrance like that one, Laurie gave every impression of being satisfied to share a joke about his father. It never occurred to me that the foundations of our parental authority were being slowly shattered until he came home from school some three or four days later with his jacket torn and an air of great innocent suffering. He was half an hour late, and he was accompanied by two of his friends, both of unsavory character; they strode manfully into the house and on into the study where my husband was peacefully doing research for an article on extinct fishes. I heard part of the conversation from upstairs where I was trying to dress Jannie after her nap. With my mind almost unoccupied, I listened without any real attention. "And they threw stones," one of Laurie's friends said in a thin, excited voice; he is somewhat older than Laurie, and he usually tells Laurie's stories for him when Laurie is too modest to tell them for himself, "and they said *terrible* language, and they *hit* Laurie, and *everything*."

"Where were *you* all this time?" my husband asked. I could feel through the floor the righteous indignation mounting in the study. "Where were you two while these boys were hitting Laurie?"

There was a moment of quiet, and then Laurie's voice: "George was behind the tree, and William was running up here to tell you." Laurie apparently stopped to think for a minute. "I didn't run," he added finally, "because I *can't* very well, in these snow pants."

The enemy–I could see them from the upstairs front window–were still lingering outside, backing down the hill slowly, prepared to do further battle. Then I heard the front door slam. My husband issued forth, supported valiantly on either side by Laurie's two friends, while Laurie, with commendable discretion, stayed just inside the front door, yelling, "Here comes my *father!*"

Halfway up the hill, the enemy waited for my husband, and, although I could not hear, I could see them—my husband speaking fiercely and the enemy looking at him with wide, honest eyes. Presently the battle was resolved; my husband turned and stamped back to the house and the enemy went on down the hill, turning at a safe distance to call inaudible insults.

When my husband came inside, I went downstairs to meet him. "Well?" I said.

All of them began talking at once. "And they *hit* Laurie and *every*thing," his talkative friend said; "They even chased *me*," his other friend added.

"And these darn old snow pants," Laurie said at the same time, while over all of them rose the voice of my husband saying, "Ought to be taught better manners. Boy like that deserves a good whipping."

Jannie came down the stairs behind me, asking hopefully, "Was Laurie bad? I'm good, aren't I? Did Laurie do something *new* bad?"

When I had isolated the various political maneuvers into offense and defense, the story went something like this: Laurie and his two friends were walking home from school, entirely without malice, not hurting anybody and minding their own business. As a matter of fact, they stopped quite of their own accord to pick up the books of a little girl who had dropped them into a mud puddle. Furthermore, they were not even thinking any harm, because they were all three most unpleasantly surprised when the largest of the enemy, a boy named David Howell, came up behind them and pulled on the hood of Laurie's jacket. When Laurie said "Hey!"—and we all agreed he was perfectly justified—David spat at him, pronounced half a dozen forbidden epithets, and finally struck him. Laurie's two friends took no active part in the battle, partly because David was bigger than any of them and partly because, as they explained at great length, they felt strongly that it was Laurie's fight and interference would not be sporting. They had come home with Laurie, however, to be his witnesses and to see that justice was done.

"What did you do to David?" I asked my husband.

"I said you'd tell his mother," he said virtuously.

I have seen David's mother, have even spoken to her at P.-T.A. meetings. She is one of those impressive women who usually head committees on supervising movics, taking the entire sixth grade on a tour of one of our local factories, or outlawing slingshots, and I daresay she would be the first person everyone would think of if there should arise an occasion for the mothers to lift the school building and carry it bodily to another location. I felt very strongly, as a matter of fact, that bringing David's mother into this incident was a grave tactical error.

But there were the four of them looking at me trustingly—five, if you count Jannie, who was saying "Poor, poor Laurie," and rubbing his head violently.

"I'll phone her right away," I said, trying to make it sound resolute and threatening. After some unavoidable fumbling with the telephone book I found the Howells' number and finally, with everyone sitting around the phone expectantly, cleared my throat, straightened my shoulders, and briskly gave the number to the operator. After a minute, a strong, no-nonsense voice said "Hello?"

"Hello," I said faintly, "is this Mrs. Howell?"

"Yes," she said. She sounded quite civil, so I changed my mind and said as politely as I could, "Mrs. Howell, I don't know if your boy David has told you about attacking my son Laurie on his way home from school today, but I thought I'd better call you anyway and see if we can't do something about it." Realizing that I had ended a little weakly, I added, "Laurie is *quite* badly hurt."

Laurie looked up, gratified, and nodded. "Tell her I'm dead," he said.

"Mrs. Howell," I said into the phone, scowling at Laurie, "I *do* think that a boy so much bigger than Laurie —a boy so much bigger, as David is—I mean, David is so much bigger than Laurie that I *do* think—"

All this time Mrs. Howell had been silent. Now she said amiably, "I quite agree with you, of course. But I can't quite believe this of David; David is such a *quiet* boy. Is your little boy sure it wasn't David Williams or David Martin?"

"Are you sure it wasn't David Williams or David Martin?" I asked hopefully of the audience beyond the telephone. They all shook their heads violently, and one of Laurie's friends—the one who ran—said enthusiastically, "I know David Howell, and it was him all right. Anyway, he's always doing things like this. Two, three times now, he's hit Laurie. And me, too. He hits everybody."

"It was certainly your David," I said to Mrs. Howell. "They all agree on that. He picked a fight with Laurie on the way home from school and really hurt Laurie *quite* badly."

"Well," she said. "I'll certainly speak to David," she added after a minute.

"Thank you," I said, perfectly content to depart with this empty triumph, but my husband said, "Tell her he was fresh to me, too."

"He was fresh to my husband, too," I said obediently into the phone.

"Really?" Mrs. Howell said, as though David were fresh to her husband all the time and this was no surprise. "Well," she said again, "I'll certainly speak to him."

"Tell her he's hit me lots of times," Laurie said.

"Don't forget the bad words," one of Laurie's friends prompted.

"Make it really forceful," my husband said. "Why should he get away with a thing like this?"

"Will you see that this is stopped once and for all?" I demanded emphatically into the phone.

Her voice sharpened. "I *said* I'd speak to David," she repeated ominously.

"Thank you," I said hastily, and hung up.

We were congratulating one another on our victory when the phone rang. "This is Mrs. Howell," she said when I answered, and her voice had lost much of its civility. "I spoke to David," she went on. "I told you I would. And it seems that David was not entirely at fault." She dwelt on the last few words as though they gave her some fierce pleasure.

"I don't understand," I said. "Laurie was just walking along the—"

"I beg your pardon," she said, still with great relish. "What about the rock he threw at David?"

I looked at Laurie over the top of the phone, and he returned my glance with sober earnestness. "What rock?" I said, and Laurie's gaze did not waver, but an odd sort of reminiscent pleasure crept into his eye.

"Laurie," said Mrs. Howell plainly, "threw a rock and hit David in the head. There's a big big bump. David hadn't done *any*thing up to then. But if your little boy throws rocks, I can hardly blame—"

I retreated abruptly to safer ground. "Surely," I said, "you are not going to say that there is *any* excuse for a bigger boy hitting a smaller boy?"

"I shall certainly speak to David about that," she said stiffly. "But then, when Laurie's father called David a little sneak and said he ought to be horsewhipped—"

"What about what David called Laurie?" I countered tellingly. "It was so bad that Laurie wouldn't dream of repeating it."

Laurie and his two friends immediately said loudly what it was.

"Your husband said David ought to be horsewhipped," she said, not shaken, and almost, I thought, as though he were not actually the first person who had suggested major punishment for David, "and poor little David tried to tell him that Laurie had been throwing rocks. You really *ought* to do something about a child throwing rocks. None of *my* children throw rocks; it's something *I* can't stand. But poor little David–"

"David did so throw rocks," I said. "And if my husband said–"

"I did not say it," my husband said.

"Surely there is no excuse," she said, "for a grown man to pick on a poor little boy."

I backed up again. "What about poor little Laurie?" I asked. "He was *quite* badly hurt. Surely there is no excuse–"

"Poor little David–" she began.

"And my poor little–" I said, and then started again. "My husband, I mean. What about the names they yelled at *him?*"

I was suddenly reminded of the time Mrs. Howell had taken part in a local debate, holding and maintaining with absolute conviction the position that our state should secede from the United States to avoid having its natural resources completely depleted. "Furthermore—" she was saying.

"What a way to bring up a child," I said gently. "What kind of a mother are you?"

My audience, I perceived, was growing restless. Laurie's two friends were putting on their overshoes; Laurie himself had entered into an elaborately casual game with Jannie that had taken them almost to the kitchen doorway, and my husband was sauntering almost noiselessly back to the study.

"Now you listen to me," Mrs. Howell began, her voice rising, "now you listen to me—"

I hung up gracefully and followed Laurie into the kitchen.

"Laurie," I said sternly, "did you throw a rock at David?"

Laurie pondered, frowning, his head on one side and one finger thoughtfully tapping his cheek. "I forget," he said at last.

"Try to remember," I said threateningly. Laurie shook his head in despair. "I just forget," he said.

I went to the study door. "Did you call David a little sneak?" I demanded.

My husband looked up from his article on extinct fishes. "A little what?" he said.

"A little sneak."

"Don't be ridiculous," my husband said. "Why would I

call what's-his-name a little sneak?" He turned back to his article. "Are you still worrying about *that?*" he asked.

The phone rang. I strode over and slammed it out of the receiver. "Well?" I said.

"If you think you can just hang up on people just because your son is a little bully and goes around throwing rocks and–"

"If you think you and your half-witted David can get away with picking on every child in the neighborhood just because he's overgrown and stupid–"

"If you would care to–"

"Perhaps *you* would like to–"

We hung up simultaneously. My husband opened the study door and looked out. "Who were you talking to?" he asked.

"Look," I said, "if you'd just take care of your own affairs and let Laurie fight his own battles and not come to me to–"

"I'm good, aren't I?" Jannie said. She came over and pulled at my hand. "I'm *good*, aren't I?"

My husband said loudly, "Let's box for a while, son. Get the gloves." Without looking at me he added, "We'll box out in the woodshed. Then," he said thoughtfully, "the noise won't bother Mother when she's on the phone."

"Aren't I?" said Jannie urgently. "*Are*n't I?"

I reached for the phone, and then hesitated. It was time to start the potatoes for dinner; I had a quick picture of Mrs. Howell peeling potatoes with one hand while she held a phone with the other, and I heard Laurie yelp as he walked into what was almost certainly a right cross.

"Want to help Mommy make dinner?" I asked Jannie.

Mrs. Howell and I met at the meat counter in the grocery the next morning; she smiled and I smiled and then she said, "How is Laurie today?"

"He seems much better, thanks," I said solemnly. "And David?"

"Fairly well," she said without turning a hair.

"Horrible little beasts," I said.

"Liars, all of them," she said. "*I* never believe a word they say."

We both laughed and turned to regard the meat. "They certainly do eat, though," she said mournfully. "I suppose it's hamburger again today."

"I was thinking about liver," I said.

"Will Laurie eat liver?" she asked with interest. "David won't touch it; do you cook it any special way?"

I REMEMBER THAT during that fall and winter Laurie was still wearing, when I forced him, a pair of red overalls onto which I had embroidered—during a time when I was somewhat more free and had a good deal more time to spend on the pretty little delicacies of life—a "Laurie" in green silk. He wore it to school only once, as I remember, and after that we made a bargain about how if I didn't make him wear it in public he would try to bring himself to it on strictly private occasions. When it began to grow noticeably short on him, without being noticeably worn, I whimsically crossed out the "Laurie" with a green embroidered line, and embroidered "Joanne" underneath, and shortened it along with half a dozen other pair of overalls for Jannie. She wore it during the late spring and early summer, when Laurie first started going to the barber to get his hair cut; she was now wearing the green corduroy jacket Laurie had worn the day we moved. This was when my personal schedule resolved itself into a round of hemlines and chocolate pudding. When I was not shortening or lengthening the one I was stirring the other. The summer saw Jannie inherit a number of pullover shirts, which are fortunately without gender, and thousands of bachelor socks, in preparation for nursery school in the fall. Laurie had a new jacket for school, which we were taught to call a windbreaker rather than a jacket, and his shoes were so huge that I was uncomfortably made aware that he had passed from the lower-priced size into the higher-priced size.

Summers go by so quickly, with a minimum of washing and a maximum of daylight, that we none of us have ever been able to perceive that infinitely cruel moment when the year turns and the days draw in; one morning the children were drinking lemonade in the back yard and talking largely of what they planned to build during the summer, and the next afternoon they were raking leaves and Jannie had lost a sandal in the leaf pile, to be hidden until perhaps next spring. Mothers have their own seasonal occupations; one afternoon I was sitting quietly in the living room, lengthening and shortening overalls in a sort of unworldly account; I had done three pair—one short and two long—when Laurie wandered in and stood in the center of the room, regarding me bleakly. Behind him trailed his dear friends Stuart and Robert, and after a few minutes, about as long as it takes short fat legs to catch up, Jannie plodded in. Our big dog Toby followed *her*. They lined themselves up in the center of the carpet and stood looking at me silently.

I looked up, forcing an expression of bright cheer onto my face. Unasked I said, "You may each have a piece of candy from the dish on the table."

"No, thank you," said Laurie gloomily.

"No, thank you," said Robert.

"No, thank you," said Stuart.

They stood sadly, watching me as I pushed the needle in and out of the cloth.

"No, thanks," said Jannie.

Laurie sighed deeply; so did Stuart and then Robert. I smiled falsely and said, "Would you each like an apple then?"

Laurie shook his head, so did Stuart and Robert and then, finally, Jannie.

"Nothing at all," said Laurie tragically. He paced over and sat down on the couch, and Robert and Stuart followed him. The three of them watched me sewing, and I tried with some embarrassment to hide what I was doing.

Toby still sat in the middle of the floor, looking with perplexed eyes first at me and then at the boys.

"Would you like to run down to the store and get some ice cream for all of us?" The boys shook their heads, as one man.

Jannie sat down solidly on the floor next to Toby and asked me, "Are you fixing Laurie's overalls?"

"Why, I certainly am," I said gaily.

"For school tomorrow?" Jannie asked.

There was a long silence. Then Laurie said, "Aaaaaah, *keep* quiet," to Jannie.

"What you talking about it for?" Stuart demanded.

"Old big-mouth Jannie," Robert said.

"Never mind, boys," I said. "You've had a fine summer."

"But *school*," Laurie said, as one to whom a vast injustice has been done.

"I know," I said. "Would you each like a cookie?"

"Naw," Laurie said.

"Why'n earth they want us to go to school *any*way?" Stuart demanded.

"Old first grade," Robert said.

"Why," I said treacherously, "first thing you know you'll be having a wonderful time in school. You've just forgotten what school is *like*."

"*No*, we haven't," Robert said.

"*I* used to *love* school," I said.

This was a falsehood so patent that none of them felt it necessary to answer me, even in courtesy. They sat and stared at me instead.

"Why don't you do something—play, or something?" I asked. "Then you'd forget all about it."

"We could play school," Jannie suggested. "Why don't we play school?"

She was silent as the three faces turned evilly towards her.

"We could ride our bikes," Robert said unenthusiastically.

"*Why* don't you?" I said, with great animation. "That would be *fun.*"

"We could have a war," Stuart said.

"We could play store," Laurie said.

"We could play school," Jannie said.

"Listen," Stuart said, "we could be Indians and Jannie could be our prisoner . . ."

"We could tie her up," Laurie said, looking at his sister speculatively.

"I will be your prisoner," Jannie said cheerfull, "and you must all tie me up and be Indians."

"No, *listen,*" Robert said. Activity came to all three of them at once. Robert rolled off the couch and ran into the hall, and the other two followed. After a minute Jannie hoisted herself off the floor and went along too. Toby, opening one eye, sighed deeply and got up; he had just started across the floor when the three boys and Jannie came hurrying back.

"Listen," Laurie said to me excitedly, "we're going to make a show. You're going to be the audience, and you got to go out in the kitchen while we get ready."

It was the last day of vacation; I put my needle carefully through the hem I was sewing and folded all the overalls and set them aside. Laurie and Robert pushed me out into the kitchen, where I took a handful of cookies and sat down, munching, to wait.

After about five minutes and much loud consultation they called me back and sat me down on the couch. Then Stuart sat in the chair I had vacated and took up the newspaper.

"I'm supposed to be reading the paper," he told me condescendingly.

Laurie and Robert and Jannie and Toby were in the dining room; I could hear them arguing. Finally there was a knock on the dining room door and Stuart put down his paper and said, "Come in." Laurie entered, wearing his cowboy hat, his spurs, his gun, his cowboy vest, his neckerchief, his lasso, and his boots. "Hi, pardner," he said.

"Hi, pardner," Stuart said.

Laurie sat down in the chair across from Stuart, and he and Stuart regarded one another intently.

"How are you, pardner?" Laurie enquired at last.

"Oh, I'm fine, pardner," Stuart said. They giggled

slightly and then Stuart, with a large expansive gesture, said, "Have some candy, pardner."

"Thanks, pardner, don't mind if I do," Laurie said. He swaggered over to the table, helped himself to a piece of candy, and went back to his chair. He finished the candy, licked his fingers and then, with a loud and dramatic groan, grasped his stomach and rolled off the chair onto the floor, where he lay still groaning. "See," he said, raising his head to look at me, "the candy was poisoned."

"I see," I said. "Very effective."

Laurie subsided, and there was a long pause, during which Stuart began to fidget, looking at the candy dish. Then finally he said, "Robert, come *on*," and Robert said from the dining room, "Okay, I'm *coming*. I got to get my *gun* on, don't I?"

Then there was another knock on the dining room door, and Stuart said "Come in."

Robert came in, said "Hi, pardner," and sat down.

"Hi, pardner," Stuart said. "Have a piece of candy."

"Don't care if I do," said Robert. He took his candy, swallowed it whole, and then fell groaning on top of Laurie.

"Now me," Jannie howled from the dining room, and she hurried in, said "Hi, pardner," over her shoulder to Stuart, and took a piece of candy. "Can I have two?" she asked me, and I shook my head no. She ate her candy, groaned shrilly, and sat on Robert.

"Guess I'll have a piece of candy too," Stuart said. He fell groaning onto the heap on the floor.

I began to applaud, and Laurie put his head up and said, "*That's* not the end."

"Sorry," I said. I started to take a piece of candy, remembered in time that it was poisoned, and drew back my hand.

Laurie disengaged himself from the pile on the floor. "Now the stagecoach," he said.

The others got up and dusted themselves off. Everybody retired to the dining room, and I waited.

Finally Laurie reappeared, leading Toby by the collar. "I'm the good cowboy," he explained to me. "I'm Hopalong Cassidy and I–"

"*I'm* Hopalong Cassidy," Robert's voice rose protestingly from the other room.

"I'm Roy Rogers," Laurie continued smoothly, "and this is the stagecoach and I'm riding along with it."

"What's the stagecoach?" I asked, confused.

"Toby is," Laurie said. Toby glanced at me in mild apology. "See," Laurie said, "the gold is in the stagecoach and the bad guys are going to try and get it, but me and my gang, we're riding close along . . ." He began to hurry Toby across the room, making galloping cowboy noises, while Toby stumbled reluctantly along behind him.

"Good dog," I said reassuringly, and Toby put his head down and galloped resolutely. "Good dog," I said.

As they passed the dining room door for the second

time the horde of bandits fell upon them. Stuart and Robert brandished their guns, shouting fearfully and making simultaneous sounds of horse hooves and gunfire. Jannie, a small stout cowboy in a flapping hat, carrying a water pistol, followed fiercely, saying "Bang," with outlaw abandon.

"We got ya covered," Hopalong Cassidy remarked. Roy Rogers, undaunted, took cover behind a chair, while the stagecoach trotted hastily over to the couch and tried to get into my lap.

Stuart and Robert had now taken cover also, one in the dining room doorway, the other in the angle of the fireplace. They were shooting across the room, taking careful aim and exposing themselves rashly before leaping back into hiding.

Jannie sat down in the middle of the floor and began to take off her sandals. "Something in my shoe," she told me. "Wait a minute, boys, till I get my shoe fixed."

"Get into a safe place," Laurie shouted at her, "you want to get killed, woman?"

"Bang," Jannie said, aiming her water pistol at him. "Bang," she said, at Stuart, and "Bang" at Robert. "I killed you all three," she said. "Now I can fix my shoe."

Laurie began to inch out from behind the chair until he was standing free of it. "Reach," he said suddenly. "Drop them guns."

Obediently, Stuart and Robert dropped their guns and raised their hands. Laurie walked over, gun ready, and frisked them both. Then he shot them. They both fell, dying fearfully. Robert raised himself on one elbow and said, "Joe, Joe."

"What, Joe?" Laurie said, turning.

"Get the guys that did this, Joe," Robert said.

"I shore will, Joe," Laurie said. He turned thoughtfully and shot Jannie, who looked up, surprised. "I said I was fixing my *shoe*," she said irritably.

"Y'got it anyway," Laurie said.

"Okay," said Jannie. She fell obligingly over onto her side and went on putting on her shoe that way.

"Well," I said, applauding again, "this has certainly been an exciting—"

"Listen," Laurie said earnestly, "this is only our *practice*. You're only seeing the *practice*, so far."

"We're going to do a real play when we finish our *practice*," Stuart confirmed.

"Reach," Laurie said to him.

"I won't," Stuart said pettishly. "Why do *I* always have to be the guy that reaches?"

"Keep them hands up," Laurie ordered. Robert stole up behind him and put a gun into his back. "*You* reach," Robert said.

Laurie dropped his gun and Stuart picked it up. Robert shot Stuart and Laurie and they both fell groaning.

"Who's the good guy," Stuart asked suddenly. "I forget."

"I'm Gene Autry," Laurie said.

"I'm Roy Rogers," Robert said.

"*I*'m the good guy, then," Stuart said with satisfaction. "Reach."

Stuart shot Robert and Laurie

"Listen," Laurie said from the floor, "we don't *die* right. We ought to roll more."

"Sometimes we ought to get dragged by our horses," Robert added.

"Reach!" Jannie said suddenly. Stunned, Gene Autry, Roy Rogers, and Hopalong Cassidy turned; Jannie had them all covered with her water pistol.

"It's a *dame*," Stuart said.

"A cowgirl," Robert amplified.

"It's Jesse James," Laurie said. "Now you must shoot us all, Jan."

"Bang, bang, bang," Jannie said, and the heroes fell, rolled, goaned, and were even dragged a little by their horses.

While they were still groaning I stole away, back into the kitchen, where I poured four glasses full of fruit juice and put cookies on a plate. When I came back into the living room the actors were dusting themselves off.

"That was a great show," I said.

"We'll do a *real* one tomorrow," Laurie said. Then his face fell. "I forgot," he said.

I thought briefly and comfortably of the quiet mornings, the long lovely afternoons, the early bedtimes.

"Well," I said, with immense heartiness, "it will be summer again before we all know it."

"A WHAT?" said Jannie.

"What *for?*" said Laurie.

EVERYONE ALWAYS SAYS the third baby is the easiest one to have, and now I know why. It's the easiest because it's the funniest, because you've been there twice, and you know. You know, for instance, how you're going to look in a maternity dress about the seventh month, and you know how to release the footbrake on a baby carriage without fumbling amateurishly, and you know how to tie your shoes before and do knee-chests after, and while you're not exactly casual, you're a little bit off-hand about the whole thing. Sentimental people keep insisting that women go on to have a third baby because they love babies, and cynical people seem to maintain that a woman with two healthy, active children around the house will do *any*thing for ten quiet days in the hospital; my own position is somewhere between the two, but I acknowledge that it leans toward the latter.

Because it *was* my third I was spared a lot of unnecessary discomfort. No one sent us any dainty pink sweaters, for instance. We received only one pair of booties, and those were a pair of rosebud-covered white ones that someone had sent Laurie when he was born and which I had given, still in their original pink tissue paper, to a friend when *her* first child was born; she had subsequently sent them to her cousin in Texas for a second baby and the cousin sent them back East on the occasion of a mutual friend's twins; the mutual friend gave them to me, with a card saying "Love to Baby" and the pink tissue paper hardly ruffled. I set them carefully aside, because I knew someone who was having a baby in June.

I borrowed back my baby carriage from my next-door neighbor, took the crib down out of the attic, washed my way through the chest of baby shirts and woolen shawls, briefed the incumbent children far enough ahead of time, and spent a loving and painstaking month packing my suitcase. This time I knew exactly what I was taking with me to the hospital, but assembling it took time and eventually required an emergency trip to the nearest metropolis. I packed it, though, finally: a yellow nightgown trimmed with lace, a white nightgown that tied at the throat with a blue bow, two of the fanciest bed-jackets I could find—that was what I went to the city for——and then, two pounds of homemade fudge, as many mystery stories as I could cram in, and a bag of apples. Almost at the last minute I added a box of pralines, a bottle of expensive cologne, and my toothbrush. I have heard of people who take their own satin sheets to the hospital, but that has always seemed to me a waste of good suitcase space.

My doctor was very pleasant and my friends were very thoughtful; for the last two weeks before I went to the hospital almost everyone I know called me almost once a day and said "Haven't you gone *yet*?" My mother- and father-in-law settled on a weekend to visit us when, according to the best astronomical figuring, I should have had a two-week-old baby ready to show them; they arrived, were entertained with some restraint on my part, and left, eyeing me with disfavor and some suspicion. My mother sent me a telegram from California saying "Is everything all right? Shall I come? Where is baby?" My children were sullen, my husband was embarrassed.

Everything was, as I say, perfectly normal, up to and including the frightful moment when I leaped out of bed at two in the morning as though there had been a pea under the mattress; when I turned on the light my husband said sleepily, "Having baby?"

"I really don't know," I said nervously. I was looking for the clock, which I hide at night so that in the morning when the alarm rings I will have to wake up looking for it. It was hard to find without the alarm ringing.

"Shall I wake up?" my husband asked without any sign of pleased anticipation.

"I can't find the *clock*," I said.

"Clock?" my husband said. "Clock. Wake me five minutes apart."

I unlocked the suitcase, took out a mystery story, and sat down in the armchair with a blanket over me. After a few minutes, Ninki, who usually sleeps on the foot of Laurie's bed, wandered in and settled down on a corner of the blanket by my feet. She slept as peacefully as my husband did most of the night, except that now and then she raised her head to regard me with a look of silent contempt.

Because the hospital is five miles from our house I had an uneasy feeling that I ought to allow plenty of time, particularly since neither of us had ever learned to drive and consequently I had to call our local taxi to take me to the hospital. At seven-thirty I called my doctor and we chatted agreeably for a few minutes, and I said I would just give the children their breakfast and wash up the dishes and then run over to the hospital, and he said that would be just fine and he'd plan to meet me later, then; the unspoken conviction between us was that I ought to be back in the fields before sundown.

I went into the kitchen and proceeded methodically to work, humming cheerfully and stopping occasionally to grab the back of a chair and hold my breath. My husband told me later that he found his cup and saucer (the one with "Father" written on it) in the oven, but I am inclined to believe that he was too upset to be a completely reliable informant. My own recollection is of doing everything the way I have a thousand times before—school-morning short cuts so familiar that I am hardly aware, usually, of doing them at all. The frying pan, for instance. My single immediate objective was a cup of coffee, and I decided to heat up the coffee left from the night before, rather than taking the time to make fresh; it seemed brilliantly logical to heat it in the frying pan because anyone knows that a broad shallow container will heat liquid faster than a tall narrow one like the coffeepot. I will not try to deny, however, that it *looked* funny.

By the time the children came down everything seemed to be moving along handsomely; Laurie grimly got two glasses and filled them with fruit juice for Jannie and himself. He offered me one, but I had no desire to eat, or in fact to do anything which might upset my precarious balance between two and three children, or to interrupt my morning's work for more than coffee, which I was still doggedly making in the frying pan. My husband came downstairs, sat in his usual place, said good-morning to the children, accepted the glass of fruit juice Laurie poured for him, and asked me brightly, "How do you feel?"

"Splendid," I said, making an enormous smile for all of them. "I'm doing wonderfully well."

"Good," he said. "How soon do you think we ought to leave?"

"Around noon, probably," I said. "Everything is fine, really."

My husband asked politely, "May I help you with breakfast?"

"No, indeed," I said. I stopped to catch my breath and smiled reassuringly. "I feel *so* well," I said.

"Would you be offended," he said, still very politely, "if I took this egg out of my glass?"

"Certainly not," I said. "I'm sorry; I can't think how it got there."

"It's nothing at all," my husband said. "I was just thirsty."

They were all staring at me oddly, and I kept giving them my reassuring smile; I *did* feel spendid; my months of waiting were nearly over, my careful preparations had finally been brought to a purpose, tomorrow I would be wearing my yellow nightgown. "I'm *so* pleased," I said.

I was slightly dizzy, perhaps. And there *were* pains, but they were authentic ones, not the feeble imitations I had been dreaming up the past few weeks. I patted Laurie on the head. "Well," I said, in the tone I had used perhaps five hundred times in the last months, "Well, do we want a little boy or a little boy?"

"Won't you sit down?" my husband said. He had the air of a man who expects that an explanation will somehow be given him for a series of extraordinary events in which he is unwillingly involved. "I think you ought to sit down," he added urgently.

It was about then that I realized that he was right. I ought to sit down. As a matter of fact, I ought to go to the hospital right now, immediately. I dropped my reassuring smile and the fork I had been carrying around with me.

"I'd better hurry," I said inadequately.

My husband called the taxi and brought down my suitcase. The children were going to stay with friends, and one of the things we had planned to do was drop them off on our way to the hospital; now, however, I felt vitally that I had not the time. I began to talk fast.

"You'll have to take care of the children," I told my husband. "See that . . ." I stopped. I remember thinking with incredible clarity and speed. "See that they finish their breakfast," I said. Pajamas on the line, I thought, school, cats, toothbrushes. Milkman. Overalls to be mended, laundry. "I ought to make a list," I said vaguely. "Leave a note for the milkman tomorrow night. Soap, too. We need soap."

"Yes, dear," my husband kept saying. "Yes dear yes dear."

The taxi arrived and suddenly I was saying goodbye to the children. "See you later," Laurie said casually. "Have a good time."

"Bring me a present," Jannie added.

"Don't worry about a thing," my husband said.

"Now, don't you worry," I told him. "There's nothing to worry about."

"Everything will be *fine*," he said. "Don't worry."

I waited for a good moment and then scrambled into

the taxi without grace; I did not dare risk my reassuring smile on the taxi driver but I nodded to him briskly.

"I'll be with you in an hour," my husband said nervously. "And don't worry."

"Everything will be *fine*," I said. "Don't worry."

"Nothing to worry about," the taxi driver said to my husband, and we started off, my husband standing on the lawn wringing his hands and the taxi tacking insanely from side to side of the road to avoid even the slightest bump.

I sat very still in the back seat, trying not to breathe. I had one arm lovingly around my suitcase, which held my yellow nightgown, and I tried to light a cigarette without using any muscles except those in my hands and my neck and still not let go of my suitcase.

"Going to be a beautiful day," I said to the taxi driver at last. We had a twenty-minute trip ahead of us, at least —much longer, if he continued his zig-zag path. "Pretty warm for this time of year."

"Pretty warm yesterday, too," the taxi driver said.

"It *was* warm yesterday," I conceded, and stopped to catch my breath. The driver, who was obviously avoiding looking at me in the mirror, said a little bit hysterically, "Probably be warm tomorrow, too."

I waited for a minute, and then I was able to say, dubiously, "I don't know as it will stay warm *that* long. Might cool off by tomorrow."

"Well," the taxi driver said, "it was sure warm *yesterday*."

"Yesterday?" I said. "Yes, that was a warm day."

"Going to be nice today, too," the driver said. I clutched my suitcase tighter and made some small sound—more like a yelp than anything else—and the taxi veered madly off to the left and then began to pick up speed with enthusiasm.

"Very warm indeed," the driver babbled, leaning forward against the wheel. "Warmest day I ever saw for the time of year. Usually this time of year it's colder. Yesterday it was *terribly*—"

"It was not," I said. "It was freezing. I can see the tower of the hospital."

"I remember thinking how warm it was," the driver said. He turned into the hospital drive. "It was so warm I noticed it right away. 'This is a warm day,' I thought; that's how warm it was."

We pulled up with a magnificent flourish at the hospital entrance, and the driver skittered out of the front seat and came around and opened the door and took my arm.

"My wife had five," he said. "I'll take the suitcase, Miss. Five and never a minute's trouble with any of them."

He rushed me in through the door and up to the desk. "Here," he said to the desk clerk. "Pay me later," he said to me, and fled.

"Name?" the desk clerk said to me politely, her pencil poised.

"Name," I said vaguely. I remembered, and told her.

"Age?" she asked. "Sex? Occupation?"

"Writer," I said.

"Housewife," she said.

"Writer," I said.

"I'll just put down housewife," she said. "Doctor? How many children?"

"Two," I said. "Up to now."

"Normal pregnancy?" she said. "Blood test? X-ray?"

"Look–" I said.

"Husband's name?" she said. "Address? Occupation?"

"Just put down housewife," I said. "I don't remember *his* name, really."

"Legitimate?"

"What?" I said.

"Is your husband the father of this child? Do you *have* a husband?"

"Please," I said plaintively, "can I go on upstairs?"

"Well, *really*," she said, and sniffed. "You're *only* having a baby."

She waved delicately to a nurse, who took me by the same arm everybody else had been using that morning, and in the elevator this nurse was very nice. She asked me twice how I was feeling and said "maternity?" to me inquiringly as we left the elevator; I was carrying my own suitcase by then.

Two more nurses joined us upstairs; we made light conversation while I got into the hospital nightgown. The nurses had all been to some occupational party the night before and one of them had been simply a riot; she was still being a riot while I undressed, because every now and then one of the other two nurses would turn around to me and say, "Isn't she a riot, honestly?"

I made a few remarks, just to show that I too was lighthearted and not at all nervous; I commented laughingly on the hospital nightgown, and asked with amusement tinged with foreboding what the apparatus was that they were wheeling in on the tray.

My doctor arrived about half an hour later; he had obviously had three cups of coffee and a good cigar; he patted me on the shoulder and said, "How do we feel?"

"Pretty well," I said, with an uneasy giggle that ended in a squawk. "How long do you suppose it will be before—"

"We don't need to worry about *that* for a while yet," the doctor said. He laughed pleasantly, and nodded to the nurses. They all bore down on me at once. One of them smoothed my pillow, one of them held my hand, and the third one stroked my forehead and said, "After all, you're *only* having a baby."

"Call me if you want me," the doctor said to the nurses as he left, "I'll be downstairs in the coffee shop."

"*I'll* call you you if I need you," I told him ominously, and one of the nurses said in a honeyed voice, "Now, look, we don't want our husband to get all worried."

I opened one eye; my husband was sitting, suddenly, beside the bed. He looked as though he were trying not to scream. "They *told* me to come in here," he said. "I was trying to find the waiting room."

"Other end of the hall," I told him grimly. I pounded on the bell and the nurse came running. "Get him out of here," I said, waving my head at my husband.

"They *told* me—" my husband began, looking miserably at the nurse.

"It's allllll right," the nurse said. She began to stroke my forehead again. "Hubby belongs right here."

"Either he goes or I go," I said.

The door slammed open and the doctor came in. "Heard you were here," he said jovially, shaking my husband's hand. "Look a little pale."

My husband smiled weakly.

"Never lost a father yet," the doctor said, and slapped him on the back. He turned to me. "How do we feel?" he said.

"Terrible," I said, and the doctor laughed again. "Just on my way downstairs," he said to my husband. "Come along?"

No one seemed actually to go or come that morning; I would open my eyes and they were there, open my eyes again and they were gone. This time, when I opened my eyes, a pleasant-faced nurse was standing beside me; she was swabbing my arm with a piece of cotton. Although I am ordinarily timid about hypodermics I welcomed this one with what was almost a genuine echo of my old reassuring smile. "Well, well," I said to the nurse. "Sure glad to see *you*."

"Sissy," she said distinctly, and jabbed me in the arm.

"How soon will this wear off?" I asked her with deep suspicion; I am always afraid with nurses that they feel that the psychological effect of a hypodermic is enough, and that I am actually being innoculated with some useless, although probably harmless, concoction.

"You won't even notice," she said enigmatically, and left.

The hypodermic hit me suddenly, and I began to giggle about five minutes after she left. I was alone in the room, lying there giggling to myself, when I opened my eyes and there was a woman standing beside the bed. She was human, not a nurse; she was wearing a baggy blue bathrobe. "I'm across the hall," she said. "I been hearing you."

"I was laughing," I said, with vast dignity.

"I heard you," she said. "Tomorrow it might be me, maybe."

"You here for a baby?"

"Someday," she said gloomily. "I was here two weeks ago, I was having pains. I come in the morning and that night they said to me, 'Go home, wait a while longer.' So I went home, and I come again three days later, I was having pains. And they said to me, 'Go home, wait a while longer.' And so yesterday I come again, I was having pains. So far they let me stay."

"That's too bad," I said.

"I got my mother there," she said. "She takes care of everything and sees the meals made, but she's beginning to think I got her there with false pretences."

"That's too bad," I said. I began to pound the wall with my fists.

"Stop that," she said. "Somebody'll hear you. This is my third. The first two—nothing."

"This is *my* third," I said. "I don't care who hears me."

"My kids," she said. "Every time I come home they say to me, 'Where's the baby?' My mother, too. My husband, he keeps driving me over and driving me back."

"They kept telling me the third was the easiest," I said. I began to giggle again.

"There you go," she said. "Laughing your head off. I wish *I* had something to laugh at."

She waved her hand at me and turned and went mournfully through the door. I opened my same weary eye and my husband was sitting comfortably in his chair. "I said," he said saying loudly, "I said, 'Do you mind if I read?' " He had the New York Times on his knee.

"Look," I said, "do I have anything to read? Here I am, with nothing to do and no one to talk to and you sit there and read the New York Times right in front of me and here I am, with nothing—"

"How do we feel?" the doctor asked. He was suddenly much taller than before, and the walls of the room were rocking distinctly.

"Doctor," I said, and I believe that my voice was a little louder than I intended it should be, "you better give me—"

He patted me on the hand and it was my husband instead of the doctor. "Stop yelling," he said.

"I'm *not* yelling," I said. "I don't like this any more. I've changed my mind, I don't want any baby, I want to go home and forget the whole thing."

"I know *just* how you feel," he said.

My only answer was a word which certainly I knew that I *knew*, although I had never honestly expected to hear it spoken in my own ladylike voice.

"Stop yelling," my husband said urgently. "*Please* stop saying that."

I had the idea that I was perfectly conscious, and I looked at him with dignity. "Who is doing this?" I asked. "You or me?"

"It's all right," the doctor said. "We're on our way." The walls were moving along on either side of me and the woman in the blue bathrobe was waving from a doorway.

"She loved me for the dangers I had passed," I said to the doctor, "and I loved her that she did pity them."

"It's all right, I tell you," the doctor said. "Hold your breath."

"Did he finish his New York Times?"

"Hours ago," the doctor said.

"What's he reading now?" I asked.

"The Tribune," the doctor said. "Hold your breath."

It was so unbelievably bright that I closed my eyes. "Such a lovely time," I said to the doctor. "Thank you so much for asking me, I can't tell you how I've enjoyed it. Next time you must come to our–"

"It's a girl," the doctor said.

"Sarah," I said politely, as though I were introducing them. I still thought I was perfectly conscious, and then I was. My husband was sitting beside the bed, smiling cheerfully.

"What happened to *you?*" I asked him. "No Wall Street Journal?"

"It's a girl," he said.

"I know," I said. "I was there."

I was in a pleasant, clean room. There was no doubt that it was all over; I could see my feet under the bedspread.

"It's a girl," I said to my husband.

The door opened and the doctor came in. "Well," he said. "How do we feel?"

"Fine," I said. "It's a girl."

"I know," he said.

The door was still open and a face peered around it. My husband, the doctor, and I, all turned happily to look. It was the woman in the blue bathrobe.

"Had it yet?" I asked her.

"No," she said. "You?"

"Yep," I said. "You going home again?"

"Listen," she said. "I been thinking. Home, the kids all yelling and my mother looking sad like she's disappointed in me. Like I did something. My husband, every time he sees me jump he reaches for the car keys. My sister, she calls me every day and if I answer the phone she hangs up. Here, I get three meals a day I don't cook, I know all the nurses, and I meet a lot of people going in and out. I figure I'd be a *fool* to go home. What was it, girl or boy?"

"Girl," I said.

"Girl," she said. "They say the third's the easiest."

TWO

I BELIEVE THAT all women, but especially housewives, tend to think in lists; I have always believed, against all opposition, that women think in logical sequence, but it was not until I came to empty the pockets of my light summer coat that year that I realized how thoroughly the housekeeping mind falls into the list pattern, how basically the idea of a series of items, following one another docilely, forms the only possible reasonable approach to life if you have to live it with a home and a husband and children, none of whom would dream of following onc another docilely. What started me thinking about it was the little slips of paper I found in the pockets of my light summer coat, one beginning "cereal, shoes to shop, bread, cheese, peanut butter, evening paper, doz doughnuts, CALL PICTURE." I showed this list to my husband, and he read it twice and said it didn't make any sense. When I told him that it made perfect sense because it followed my route up one side of the main street of our town and down the other side—I have to buy the cereal at a special store, because that's the only one which carries the kind the children like—he said then what did CALL PICTURE mean? and when I explained that it meant I must call the picture-framer before I started out and was in big letters because if I took the list out in the store and found I had forgotten to call the picture-framer I would then have to stop in and see him, he sniffed and said if he managed his filing cabinet the way I managed my shopping. . . . The other list I found in my summer coat pocket started out "summer coat to clnrs."

The fact that I hadn't *taken* my summer coat to the cleaners (oh, those first fall days, with the sad sharpness in the air and the leaves bright so that our road is a line of color, and the feeling of storing-in against the winter, and the pumpkins) does not materially affect my conviction that the kind of progress from one thing to another which makes up a list is deeply logical, if ineffectual. Say to my next-door neighbor that you admire her new kitchen linoleum, and she will tell you, "Do you like it, really? I wanted to get white instead of blue, but it gets dirty so quickly, and then of course John always did like blue best, but of course the cannister set and the kitchen table are lighter blue, and it would have meant replacing *them*, but then the curtains . . ." From here she may go off onto any of several tangents (I am assuming, of course, that she is not interrupted by my telling of my own experiences, or

John's saying how about bringing out some crackers and cheese for everybody, or a child crying somewhere upstairs), such as the dirt detour; she may give you a list of things which *do* get dirty (". . . a black linoleum, and do you know it showed every single track . . .") or things which do *not* get dirty (". . . and even though it was really a pale yellow it just wiped off . . ."), or she may become interested in kitchen fixtures (". . . and she had the *prettiest* curtains, but they were sort of odd, I thought, in a *kitchen;* they were . . .") or bathroom fixtures (". . . and they had the same tiles in the bathroom, only these were pink, and the curtains *there* . . .") or even John's likes and dislikes (". . . but of course he won't eat anything with garlic in it, so I have to take all the recipes I get and put in . . .").

I think that may be why my summer coat never got to the cleaners. You can start from any given point on a list and go off in all directions at once, the world being as full as it is, and even though a list is a greatly satisfying thing to have, it is extraordinarily difficult to keep it focussed on the subject at hand. Right at this point, for instance, I was thinking about demitasse cups. I personally prefer a double-sized coffee cup, but with those tiny cups coffee is served so graciously (I see a list here, going on off into tiny spoons, and after-dinner liqueurs, and me in a long gown at the table, and everyone speaking wittily, and the children sweetly asleep in the nursery with an efficient Nanny on guard)—so easily (this list includes a maid and a butler to wash the cups and polish the tiny spoons) and so elegantly (years ago my mother promised me a silver coffee service, and then there's always the coffee table we inherited from Great-Aunt Martha, and if my husband would just get to work and sand it down and varnish it . . .) that, infected as I am by the constant desire to change everything, I may give in to the demitasse, after all. What persuaded me to think about demitasse cups at all was a statement made recently by one of my close friends, who said that she personally did not like our big cups for dinner coffee, but preferred a demitasse because she liked her coffee scalding hot. That, of course, sent me off onto several tangents on *her* housekeeping; she is a *very* good friend, and I would not for the world mention to her that the last time we visited there, there was no soap in the bathroom. I am terribly fond of her, but it *is* true that her guest room windows do not open. She is a grand girl, and if she likes her coffee in small cups at my house, she shall have it that way, in spite of the fact that the last time we dined there I found a spider in the salad.

Perhaps—following still another list—if we did have demitasse cups, our after-dinner hour, which is complicated by the presence of children coming out of bathtubs, and children with pressing problems in elementary reading, and dishes on the table waiting to be washed, and dogs and cats clamoring for their supper—perhaps our after-dinner hour would somehow become imperceptibly more gracious; perhaps the children, seeing us endlessly refilling our demitasse cups, would tiptoe thoughtfully away from the dining room door. Perhaps if we had demitasse cups a local couple, who have no children and have exhibited a vast distaste for our hospitality, would come to call. Perhaps, as a matter of fact, if we had demitasse cups, we could overlook the fact that the vast distaste of the local couple was provoked by our short-tempered reception of their resentment of our children. We *should* live more graciously, after all.

Then, naturally, there is the question of the cups themselves. I am immediately tempted to buy them just as cheaply as possible (*there's* a list for you, the prices of things) and have thought of the five and ten (". . . and I got the *sweetest* little cups right there, can you imagine, and even though the cups and saucers came separately I didn't really pay much *more* . . .") but dismissed the idea through pride (". . . and everyone could *tell* because of course those *same* patterns . . ."). I shall have to go off and purchase them in some big store where I have a charge account (". . . a charge account? Let me just tell you what happened to *me* when . . .") and I suspect that I will end up after a day of shopping with four cheap flowered demitasse cups and a set of dishes (I have *so* been needing dishes) and a set of glassware which will be wonderful for the children to use when they have company for breakfast, and while I am in that department I think I ought to look at electric mixers because it is only four months to my birthday.

I tabulated recently a conversation, or double-listing, between two women, one of them me. The conversation began, civilly enough, with a compliment from me about my friend's new slipcover, which she had made herself. We then went rapidly through slipcovers (custom-made, prices of) the value of a sewing machine, the clothes children wore to school, and children's shoes (prices of). She then remarked that she hated to repeat cute things her children had said, but she just *had* to tell me what her daughter said the other day. I retaliated with a really clever story about Jannie. She said that prices were awful, weren't they; the conversation could have ended right there, with both of us crying, but fortunately one of our husbands stepped in with a remark about how we *had* really planned to play bridge, hadn't we? because if we *had*, here were the cards dealt and the chairs ready. We sat down, and she told me about how angry her husband had been the last time we played bridge, because she had reneged twice, and I told her a little sad story about how my husband had opened once with two hearts and I had said two spades and he said three diamonds and there I sat with the king, jack, seven of diamonds and . . . well, *she* told *me* about these people they used to know, and *I* told *her* about these people *we* used to know, and then she said, well, the way some people bring up their children, and I told her about the bad manners of the children of these friends of ours, and she said well, of course, progressive education, and my husband said were we going to play bridge or weren't we?

So then she said that she loved my new blouse and I said I wished I could make things for myself, and she said the stores were awful, weren't they. I told her about how a salesclerk was so rude I walked out without buying anything, and she said that the butcher in our mutual grocery was really terribly mean today about the hamburger. I said that even hamburger was almost out of our range these days and she told me about how prices are up at least two cents a pound since practically yesterday. I told her that I understood that the main reason they had given up school lunches was the cost, and she said that it really cost less to make lunch at home and send it, the way things were these days. I said the only trouble was, Laurie preferred sandwiches made with cold meat, and she said had I tried this new spread made with olives. When I said no, she said that she had also tried a new cake mix and it was marvelous, but of course you really *needed* an electric mixer, and I said my birthday was only four months off. My husband bid three hearts in a loud voice. I bid three spades, and said that I envied her the cookies she made, that my children preferred to stop off for cookies at her house because our cookies were all store-bought. She said shyly that she had made a new kind of lemon meringue tart to serve after our bridge game and my husband said oh, were we playing bridge? Her husband then bid four hearts, she bid four no trump, and I said that I was planning to get a set of demitasse cups.

We played the hand in six spades, and made it easily, but

it turns out that if I *am* going to get an electric mixer I shall have to shop around and get a really good one; she has a friend who used hers once and it fell apart. Of course she got a new one right away from the manufacturers, but my husband believed that if his partner had led anything except the ace of hearts . . . I took the recipe for the lemon meringue tarts, and when I got home I made a new list, which began "lemons, demitasse cups, summer coat to cleaners . . ."

That summer coat was a good one; I had worn it my last two years in college and every summer since. With three small children I perceived clearly what I had suspected when I had only one child, and half-believed when I had only two children—that parents must automatically resign themselves to wearing every article of their own clothing at least two years beyond its normal life expectancy. During the long summers—which are hotter, by the way, than they used to be when I was a child, just as the winters are colder—I can get along nicely on my summer coat and my few surviving cotton dresses, but the winter is another thing; unless I find someone who can fix the pockets of my old fur coat I shall not even be able to carry a handkerchief any more, unless I pin it to the front of me the way I do with Jannie. However, mending a fur coat is so ridiculous in the middle of summer that I have a little list, in my top dresser drawer, which has been there for—I think—two years. "Mend fr coat," it says.

By the time I woke up on a summer morning—the alarm having missed fire again, for the third time in a week—it was already too hot to move. I lay in bed for a few minutes, wanting to get up but unable to exert the necessary energy. From the girls' room, small voices rose in song, and I listened happily, thinking how pleasant it was to hear a brother and two sisters playing affectionately together; then, suddenly, the words of the song penetrated into my hot mind, and I was out of bed in one leap and racing down the hall. "Baby ate a spider, Baby ate a spider," was what they were singing.

Three innocent little faces were turned to me as I opened the door. Laurie, in his cowboy-print pajamas, was sitting on top of the dresser beating time with a coat hanger. Jannie, in pink pajama pants and her best organdy party dress, was sitting on her bed. Sally peered at me curiously through the bars of her crib and grinned, showing her four teeth.

"What did you eat?" I demanded. "What do you have in your mouth?"

Laurie shouted triumphantly. "A spider," he said. "She ate a spider."

I forced the baby's mouth open; it was empty. "Did she *swallow* it?"

"Why?" Jannie asked, wide-eyed. "Will it make her sick?"

"*Jannie* gave it to her," Laurie said.

"*Laurie* found it," Jannie said.

"But she ate it herself," Laurie said hastily.

I went wearily back into my own room, resisted the strong temptation to get back into bed, and began to dress. The conversation from the children indicated that they, too, were what might be called dressing.

"Put it on Baby," Laurie remarked.

"It's too little," Jannie objected.

"That's all right," Laurie said. "Put it on her anyway."

"She can wear my bluuuuuuuue shirt," Jannie said.

"*That* shirt's no good," Laurie said.

"It is so," Jannie said.

"It is not," Laurie said.

"It is so," Jannie said.

"It is not," Laurie said.

"Children," I called, my voice a little louder than it usually is at only nine in the morning. "Please stop squabbling and get dressed."

"*Laurie* started it," Jannie called back.

"*Jannie* started it," Laurie called.

Hastily I pushed the comb through my hair and hurried down the hall; hurrying made me hotter. I lifted Sally out of her crib and set her on Jannie's bed to dress her, and Laurie and Jannie immediately abandoned their dressing and came to sit on the bed and watch. I changed Sally with the casual speed that comes to mothers of three, decided against putting anything more than a diaper on her, and started downstairs with her under my arm. Behind me Jannie lifted her voice tearfully.

"I can't find my shooooooes," she howled.

Laurie began to chuckle maliciously. I saw that he was putting Jannie's red sandals on his own feet, reflected briefly and bitterly on the theory that seven-year-olds have good days and bad days, and said briskly, "Just for that, you can put Jannie's shoes on *her* feet, and buckle them for her, too."

I knew immediately what he was going to do, and, with speed, I made a strong tactical retreat downstairs before I could see him do it. In the kitchen it was hotter than ever, and I set Sally in her high chair and began opening windows and doors to get some air. The bright sunlight reassured me; by ten o'clock breakfast would be done with, I would have had my coffee; I might even feel like taking the children swimming, or on a picnic. Acting with all the alertness and vivid grace which I usually bring to the breakfast hour, I filled the coffee pot and set it on the stove, filled Sally's bottle and put it on to heat, and then looked around for Phoebe. Phoebe was our household help, and, being a local girl, she possessed all the native Vermonter's independence of thought and action; she was supposed by me to arrive every morning by eight o'clock and frequently arrived, having clearly established her emancipated state, by nine. This morning there was no sign of her, not even in her favorite spot for mornings when I get up late, which is out on the side porch playing solitaire. I began to set the table irritably.

Laurie came bounding heavily down the stairs, with Jannie's infuriated wail following him.

"Where's Phoebe?" he demanded.

"Not here yet," I said briefly, because I could not trust myself to speak fully. "Dime if you set the table."

Laurie began to sing loudly, and rattled the silverware vigorously. As his singing grew louder, a suspicion grew in me. "Did you brush your teeth?" I asked him.

He sang more sweetly still. "Did you brush your *teeth?*" I said.

The phone rang. Because I was on the wrong side of the table, and hampered by the chairs, Laurie beat me to it by a full five feet.

"Hello?" he said politely, as he has been taught. "This is Laurence." His eyes circled meaningfully around to me and he looked sorrowful. "No," he said sadly, "she's not up yet. She's still asleep."

"Young man," I said ominously, and he backed away so I could not reach the phone. "I'll tell her when she wakes up," he said, and hung up hastily. "I knew you wouldn't want to talk to *her*," he said. "She always talks so long, and you're so busy with breakfast and everything."

"Who?" I asked.

"I'll write it down for you," Laurie said. He took the telephone pad and pencil and began, with his laborious printing. The coffee boiled over, and I fled back into the kitchen. I turned off the coffee, gave Sally her bottle—she is learning to drink her milk from a cup, but insists also upon having her bottle, full, for no better apparent reason than as a weapon with which to brain anyone foolish enough to bring a head near her—and began to break eggs into a bowl. Jannie came downstairs with a clatter, her shoes, as I had known inevitably they would be, on the wrong feet.

"Where's Phoebe?" she said.

"She didn't come today," Laurie said. "Mommy's *terrible* mad. Mommy's probably going to kill her."

"Laurie," I said, but they had already started, "Mommy's going to kill Phoebe, Mommy's going to kill Phoebe."

My husband came downstairs without that spring in his step which is usually associated with daddies coming down to a good nourishing breakfast with their kiddies; he came into the kitchen and glanced around. "Where's Phoebe?" he said.

"Not here," I said.

"Mommy's going to kill Phoebe," the children chanted.

"You'll really *have* to fire that girl," my husband observed. "Good morning, children."

"*Good* morning, Daddy," Jannie said sweetly.

"*Good* morning, Dad," Laurie said manfully.

I turned around. Jannie was balancing the fruit juice glasses one on top of another. Laurie was making a train of knives and forks. Sally finished with her bottle abruptly and threw it on the floor.

"It's hot," my husband remarked. He sat down at the table, rescued a knife and fork from Laurie and a glass of fruit juice from Jannie. "Why do you let the children play with things on the table?" he asked. "Don't they have enough toys of their own?"

I did not feel equal to answering. I put the eggs, the toast, and the coffee on the table and sat down; I could tell by looking that my coffee was going to be too hot and it was perfectly clear that the toast was burned.

"What's this junk?" Laurie said, regarding his plate.

"Once," Jannie observed, through a mouthful of egg, "once there was a little boy and he had no mother or father and he ran out into the middle of the street."

"What happened to him?" Laurie asked with interest.

"He was eaten by a truck," Jannie said demurely.

"*That's* no good," Laurie said.

"It is too," Jannie said.

"It is not," Laurie said.

The phone rang. I was cornered behind Sally's high-chair and Laurie beat me again. "This is Laurence," we could hear him saying precisely. "Who is calling, please?"

He came into the kitchen and addressed his father. "It's Mr. Feeley," he said. "He wants to know can you play poker tonight."

My husband avoided looking at me. "Tell him I'll call him back," he said.

"Once there was a little boy," Jannie said, "and he had no mother or father."

"What happened to him?" I asked dutifully, Laurie being still on the phone.

"He was eaten by a bear," Jannie said. "Can I have some candy when I finish my breakfast?"

Each of the children had a toy filled with candy which sat on the table; they were little glass airplanes, and the candy inside was the sort usually used for cake decoration, tiny little colored balls of sugar. This candy enchanted Jannie, although Laurie was cynically aware that the whole amount contained in the airplane was hardly worth one chocolate-covered pepperment.

"If you eat every single bite of your breakfast," I said, "you may have some of your candy."

"Once there was a little boy," Jannie said, shoving her egg around the plate with the handle of her fork, "and he had no mother or father."

"What happened to him?" Laurie said, sliding into his chair. "He says call back before two," he remarked confidentially to his father.

"He was eaten by a elephant," Jannie said. "Look, no more breakfast."

I lifted her plate and, with a spoon, gathered the egg off the table and put it back onto the plate. "Every bite," I said firmly, "or no candy."

"Once there was a little boy," Jannie said mournfully, "and he had no mother or father."

She waited for a minute, but no one spoke; Laurie was engaged with his toast, I was trying to get Sally's spoon out of her mouth, and my husband was counting the money in his wallet.

" 'Once there was a little boy,' " Jannie said loudly, " 'and he had no mother or father,' I said."

"What happened to him?" Laurie asked resignedly.

Jannie giggled. "He was eaten by a bicycle," she said.

"Through," Laurie announced suddenly. "See?" He turned his plate upside down, his milk cup upside down on top of that, and balanced his fruit juice glass on top of the whole thing.

"Laurence," his father said absently, "your napkin is on the floor."

Laurie snatched his airplane full of candy, and retired. I picked his napkin up off the floor, unloaded the milk cup and the fruit juice glass, caught Jannie's plate just as it was sliding off the edge of the table, rescued the spoon from Sally, and said "More coffee?" to my husband.

He looked deeply into his cup. "Yes, please," he said.

Breakfast was nearly over.

Laurie had emptied his candies into a small bowl, and was stirring them around vigorously. "Look," he said, coming around to Jannie's side of the table, "Look, whirlpools."

"I want my candy," Jannie said immediately.

"Look, whirlpools," Laurie said to his father. "Whirlpools," he said to me. An idea struck him suddenly and he took a handful of the candies and put them on the tray of Sally's high chair; they rolled back and forth and Sally regarded them dubiously.

"Eat, Sally," Laurie said. "Eat, eat, eat, eat, eat, eat, eat, eat . . ."

"Laurence," I said feverishly.

"Okay, okay," Laurie said. "Look, Sally. Candy."

He pointed to the small candies and Sally tried experimentally to pick one up. Her fingers were not well enough controlled to take hold of it, and she began to giggle, chasing the candies around the highchair tray.

"Listen," Laurie shouted, "Phoebe's coming."

"Phoebe's coming," Jannie agreed loudly. She began to struggle, and Laurie at the same time tried to gather his airplane and candy together preparatory for a dash at the door. Jannie teetered backward in her chair, Laurie crashed into her, and they both went over, Jannie's plate, with egg, moving gracefully off the table after them.

"Can I have my candy now?" Jannie asked me, looking up hopefully from the floor. "*Laurie* did it."

"Phoebe," Laurie was shouting from the front door, "Mommy's going to *kill* you, and Daddy says—"

The phone rang. This time I made it first, and, breathing hard, I lifted the receiver and said "Hello?"

"Hello?" said a high thin voice. "May I please speak to Laurence?"

PHOEBE WAS THE last, for a long, long time, of my adjuvants. Not that I can't *use* help around the house, but I am, not to put too fine a point on it, the person to whom the almost unemployable slack-jawed mother's helper gravitates as to a natural home. I have never in my life made any pretence at being an efficient housekeeper; I can make a fair gingerbread and I know a thing or two about onion soup, but beyond the most rudimentary sweepings and dustings I am not capable. Not for me the turned sheet, the dated preserve, the fitted homemade slipcover or the well-ironed shirt. Nor do I stack up particularly well in the hired girl department; in our town the employer (obviously a staunch New England type who because of a broken leg or some incurable malady has found it necessary to "get help") is expected to "work along," to check dirt, to remain, at all times, level-headed.

That is why I always end up with people like Phoebe. If she could make chowder or raised doughnuts she would, in our town, have a home of her own. If she had a natural gift for getting things clean, or an instinctive ability at getting three rebellious children into bed, she would be gainfully employed in our nearest big town. If she knew how to do anything right at all, she would not be working for me.

Take Hope, for instance. I always get hold of these people because they answer an ad I put in the paper, and someone apparently read it to Hope. I wanted to phrase the ad in some cute irresistible fashion such as "I am almost helpless around a house. I honestly don't know a *thing* about housework. Isn't there some kind girl who wants to help me, at a moderate salary?" Instead, at a dollar for ten words for three days, what I usually say is "Houseworker wanted. Good ref. Mod. sal. Children. Meals. Laundry. Cleaning."

I always hire the first person who comes, usually without remembering to check on the good ref. This is not only because I am extremely gullible, but at least partially because I am openly terrified of anyone who looks me straight in the eye and speaks emphatically, and these women, looking for jobs at mod. sal. and with no serious intentions whatsoever about Meals. Laundry. Cleaning., alway use a voice of great clarity and strength when talking to me. I am usually not able to say anything at all, or else what I do say comes out entirely wrong, and modest disclaimers turn out to be flat denials—a statement to the effect that no one can cook for my husband except me because he has odd ideas about food turns out to say that I intend to do all the cooking myself, in spite of what my ad said, with the rider that I have a crazy husband who lives exclusively on bread and water.

The only person, by the way, whom I ever escaped in a situation like that was a gentlewoman of about two hundred years who came one day in answer to one of my usual ads; I tried to conduct the interview with gravity, and she answered all my timid questions with modesty and restraint until I mentioned, in the laughing voice that I reserve for controversial subjects, that dishes were a problem in a family the size of ours, particularly, I added, washing them.

"Dishes," she said eagerly, "now, I *love* dishes."

"I suppose you collect them?" I asked, for want of anything better to say.

"Washing dishes," she said. "Now, washing dishes I can't stop. If I don't watch myself—" she cackled delightedly "—I just go on washing dishes over and over and over and over and over and over again, all day long. All day *long*, now," and she cackled again.

I told her I would let her know about the job, and after she had left I telephoned the number she gave me and left a message that I had just had word that my mother was coming to live with me and so I wouldn't need anyone to help around the house.

I passed up that nice old lady, who was essentially agreeable and had at least one cleanly virtue, to hire Hope. Hope disliked washing dishes, but she did them. She wore neat house dresses, although she had a weakness for high-heeled, ankle-strap black sandals around the house. She did not quarrel with my cooking for my husband, although, as it turned out, it was unnecessary; Hope spent most of her time in the kitchen making biscuits which were light and pleasant, and cheese soufflés, and chocolate cakes, and fried chicken. I even checked her good ref. The old lady to whom I spoke was enthusiastic in her praise. "She's a *good* girl," the old lady said insistently—perhaps I feel now, *too* insistently. "You don't need to worry about Hope any, she's a *good* girl. Don't you pay any attention to what you may *hear*—that Hope is a *good* girl."

The only trouble with Hope was that she disappeared at the end of the first week, taking with her her salary, ten dollars she had borrowed from me, and my overshoes. Two days after Hope disappeared I answered a ring at the door, and found standing there a lady of unequivocal firmness and a most suspicious eye. "Is Hope here?" she asked me.

"She is not," I said shortly, not overanxious to dwell lengthily upon the subject of Hope.

"I'm her parole officer," the woman said. "If you know where she is it's your duty to tell me."

"She's got my overshoes, wherever she is," I said, and tried to close the front door, but the parole officer put her shoulder against the frame and said, "It's your civic duty as a citizen to report this matter." After I had told her all about Hope and my overshoes I pointed out that the ten dollars was relatively unimportant but that with this constant wet weather it was hard going without anything on my feet, and asked nervously what chance there was of getting them back.

"*We*'ll get them," she said enigmatically, "they can't get far without stealing a car."

A week later I was invited to the local jail to see Hope, who gave me back my overshoes with an apology for having kept them so long, asked kindly after the children, the cats, and the dog, remarked parenthetically that she had never really gotten to know my husband, and asked me to go five thousand dollars bail for her.

I told her civilly enough that these constant ads in the paper made such a drain on my pocketbook that I had really nothing left for more than household expenses, and asked nicely what she was in for. It turned out to be grand larceny; my overshoes, she said, she had never regarded as anything but a loan; it was a difficulty with a former employer's fur coat which worried her now. I shook hands cordially with the jailer's wife, declined a piece of fresh-made sponge cake, and departed. I sent a carton of cigarettes and some magazines to the jail for Hope about a month later, and got back an earnest letter saying she would be sure to come back to work for us when she got out, and could we wait three years?

Between the time I last saw Hope and the time I got her letter, Amelia had come and gone. Amelia had been recommended to me by a neighbor, with the specific statement that Amelia was not an intelligent girl, but she was able, my neighbor was confident, to do simple household tasks. Amelia washed dishes, but not very clean. She arrived every morning on foot, by a process which required that she inquire at every house in the neighborhood each day before she found ours. She never tried to borrow my overshoes, which I was keeping anyway in the only closet in the house which locked, and I sincerely believe that after working for us for two days she was still unable to find her way from the kitchen to the front door without falling over the furniture.

Like Hope, Amelia had but one major failing. The second day she was with us—which turned out, coincidentally, to be the last—she made cookies, spending all one joyous afternoon in the kitchen, droning happily to herself, fidgeting, cluttering, measuring.

At dinner, dessert arrived with Amelia's giggle and a flourish. She set the plate of cookies down in front of my husband, and my husband, who is a nervous man, glanced down at them and dropped his coffee cup. "Sinner," the cookies announced in bold pink icing, "Sinner, repent."

Phoebe did not stay with us much longer than Amelia had. She was accustomed to arriving mornings on a motorcycle, but after two weeks her mother called one morning to say that there had been an American Legion convention in a nearby city and that Phoebe was now in Kansas City. It was terribly hot all that summer, and I kept thinking about poor old Phoebe in Kansas City on her motorcycle. Perhaps I privately envied the motorcycle, it being a species of abandoned travel with which I am respectably unfamiliar; perhaps the notion of wild noisy motion appealed to Laurie. He asked me one morning later that summer, "Why don't we have a car?" I was stirring chocolate pudding—a talent of the late Phoebe's—at the stove, and he was painting at the kitchen table. Jannie was laboriously dressing her doll on the floor, singing quietly to herself while she stuffed the doll's arms brutally into one of the baby's nightgowns.

"Why don't we have a car?" I repeated absently. "I suppose because no one around here can drive."

"If we had a car," Laurie said, in the tone which I was beginning to recognize as one all seven-year-old boys use to their mothers, as of one explaining a relatively uncomplicated situation to a sort of foolish creature, apt to become sentimental and impertinent unless firmly held in check, "if we had a car, we could ride around."

"But no one around here can drive," I said.

"And we could go anywhere we wanted," Laurie said. "And we wouldn't have to walk, or drive with other people, or take taxis."

"Who would drive us?"

"I could sit in the front seat," Laurie said, "and Jannie and Sally could sit in the back seat." He thought. "And Daddy could ride on the running board."

"What would I be doing?" I asked. "Driving?"

"I want to ride in the front," Jannie said, lifting her head to scowl at her brother. "I want to ride in the front and Laurie in back with Baby."

"I'm going to ride in the front," Laurie said. "I'm older."

"But I'm a girl," Jannie said, undeniably.

"But who would *drive?*" I said.

"Listen," Laurie said to me, a thin edge of contempt in his voice, "can't you drive a *car?*"

"No, I can not."

"Can Daddy?"

"No."

"Can't *either* of you drive?"

"No."

Laurie put his paint brush down and looked at me for a long minute. "Then what *can* you do?" he asked.

"Well," I said, "I can make chocolate pudding, and I can wash dishes, and I can . . ."

"*Any*body can do that," Laurie said. "What *I* mean is, can't you drive a *car?*"

"No," I said sharply, "I can not drive a car. And I do not, furthermore, intend to learn. And I also do not want to hear one more—"

"If we had a car," Jannie said, "I could ride in the front and Laurie could ride in the back with Baby."

"I'm older," Laurie said mechanically. "*You* ride in back."

"I'm a girl," Jannie said.

"Why not let Baby ride in front?" I asked in spite of myself. "She's younger. And she's a girl."

"But if Laurie and I rode in back we would fight," Jannie said.

"That's true," I said. "So why not—" but the chocolate pudding thickened and I had to stop talking.

Jannie began to sing one of her morning songs. "On earth, what are you doing," she sang softly, "on earth, what are you doing? I am going splickety-splot. On earth, what are you doing, on earth, what are you doing? I am going thumpety-thump. We do dig and it does rain." While she sang she rocked her doll, Laurie painted amiably, and I hummed to myself while I poured the pudding into dishes and wondered whether I could get away with chicken soup again for lunch today.

Jannie began her song for the third time, and Laurie set his page aside and asked absently, "Why did you say we don't have a car?"

"We don't have a car," I said wearily, "because both Daddy and I would rather roller-skate."

"Can Daddy drive?" Jannie asked. "Daddy can do anything, can't he?"

I hesitated, not at the moment able to find an answer, and Laurie said, "If we had a car you could take us for rides."

"Now listen to me, both of you," I began with great firmness, but at that moment the baby woke up and as I started upstairs I heard Laurie asking dreamily, "Jannie, what would you do if a snake came and ate you?"

In our family a conversation such as this one about the car does not end, ever. At dinner that night Laurie remarked to his father, "Mommy is going to get a car and drive it around."

"And I'm going to ride in front," Jannie said.

"*I*'m going to ride in front," Laurie said. "I'm–"

"I'm a girl," Jannie said.

My husband regarded me with mild surprise. "A car?" he said, perplexed. "You mean, drive me if I wanted to go for a haircut? And I wouldn't have to–"

"Wait," I said, "wait, wait."

"I'm going to ride in *front*," Laurie said.

"I'm a—"

"*I* am going to ride in front," my husband said flatly.

THE MAN FROM the driving school was named Eric, and he was about eighteen years old and undisguisedly amused at meeting anyone who could not drive a car. When I told him sharply that in his business he must meet quite a few people who could not drive a car he laughed and said that usually people my age did not try to learn new tricks. I eyed the dual-control car he had parked in our driveway and said falsely that I might surprise him by learning faster than he expected. He patted me on the shoulder and said, "That's my girl."

Laurie and Jannie and my husband holding the baby stood on the front porch cheering and waving as I rode off with Eric, crushed into a corner of the seat to avoid touching any of the dual controls, and desperately afraid that if I did the car would go out of control and rocket madly off the road, no doubt killing other innocent people and very probably ending my driving lessons. Laurie and Jannie and my husband holding the baby were again on the front porch cheering, two hours later, when I came back with Eric, dismayed and bewildered and not prepared to take levelly any childish prattle about how we would drive around when we had a car.

I took ten lessons from Eric, including lessons in stopping and starting, making a U turn—that was how I got the dent in the back of the car, but Eric said they were insured against that kind of thing—making right turns and left turns, shifting gears, backing and filling, allemande left, and reeling and writhing and fainting in coils. He neglected to teach me how to turn on the lights and what to do when a funny little noise started somewhere inside. Every time I got out of his car in front of my own house, weak-kneed and with my hands stiffened into a permanent grasp on a steering wheel, I was greeted with cheers and friendly criticism by my faithful family. I completely captivated one of Laurie's friends—a young gentleman from Cub Scouts whose mother and father both know how to drive, and have for years—by running smack into the stone wall at the foot of our garden, something no one else has so far been able to do, since the wall is set approximately seven feet from the driveway and is clearly visible. Evenings, I studied a little book Eric had sold me, which told in graphic detail what to do in case the car skidded out of control, what to do in case the steering wheel came off in my hands (from this I got the vivid impression of running the car like a bobsled, and steering by leaning from side to side), and how to bandage a compound fracture.

My test, which I shall always believe was supposed to be a test of whether or not I could drive a car, I passed seemingly without effort, and with only one bad moment when, told to stop completely halfway up a hill which may well have been Mount Everest, I realized that the head inquisitor assumed with infinite amusement that I would be able to start again. He was a very patient man, and waited for several minutes, tapping his fingers gently against the window while I scoured my mind for Eric's directions on starting a car on a hill. ("Swing your wheel sharp? Turn down your lights? Keep one foot on the clutch and one foot on the brake and one foot on the starter . . . ?") "Well?" said the inquisitor, looking at me evilly.

I gestured competently with one hand, keeping the other one locked to the wheel in some obscure belief that only my grip on the wheel kept the car from rolling back down the hill. "State law," I said carelessly. "Child coming, can't start."

He glanced at me briefly and then craned his neck out of the window to see where a boy about twenty was sauntering down the sidewalk. I had hoped to distract his attention, and did, but I then discovered that it is not possible to be surreptitious about starting a stalled car on a hill. I firmly believe that the inquisitor gave me a license only because he was sure I could never start a car and so could never become a substantial menace on the highways.

Meanwhile, it had been decided who was to ride in front (Baby), I had learned to drive, the lessons had been paid for, and I had a little piece of official paper saying that I knew how to drive. We lacked only a car. This was adjusted by a gentleman who, saying he acted only from pure friendship, sold us one of *his* cars. He said he was very reluctant to part with it, particularly at that price, he said it was a better car than any of the new ones on the market, he praised its spark plugs and its birdlike appetite for oil.

"The cigarette lighter doesn't work," I pointed out in a spirit of pure critical inquiry.

"Neither does the clock," said my husband.

"And the fender is sort of caved in," I added.

"Tell you what I'll do," the man said. "I'll pay for the license plates."

"Better get that cigarette lighter fixed right away," my husband told me, as we surveyed our new car. "And the clock. Best to be on the safe side."

"I'll have to find a place to get them fixed," I said.

"Can't be too careful," my husband said.

I got into the car and reasoned out how to start it and drove with great caution, in the middle of the road, to a garage that could be reached without a left turn, and there I talked for quite a while with a young man covered with grease and oil who had "Tony" written across the front of him in big red letters. "Got a nice car there," he said, after I had told him we had just bought it, and what we paid for it, and had added trustingly that I had just learned to drive and had never before owned a car and knew nothing about cars or motors or, as a matter of fact, driving. "You're even going to have to tell me what gas to use," I added laughingly.

Tony nodded soberly. "But you got a real nice car there," he insisted, "for the price you paid, you couldn't get a better one. Needs a little attention, of course." He laughed. "Wouldn't be a car if it didn't," he told me.

"Yes, I know," I said. "The cigarette lighter–"

"You take that clutch, for instance," Tony said. He opened the door and pushed the pedal up and down reflectively. "Now I guess you don't know anything about the clutch, do you?" he asked. I shook my head, and he went on, "Well, it's a funny thing about the clutch. You go along for maybe one, two thousand miles and then all of a sudden . . ." He shrugged expressively. "You got a repair job costs you maybe two, three hundred dollars. Always better to get the clutch fixed in time, saves you money, expense, wear and tear."

"You mean I have to get something fixed?"

He shrugged again. "You don't *need* to, of course," he said. "But you got to look at it this way. You got small children, you're driving them around in the car, you're not going to take chances with *them*."

Nervously I agreed that I was not going to take chances with my small children.

"Well, then," said Tony. "Now brakes are important, too." He pushed the brake pedal down and shook his head sadly. "That guy sold you this car," he said.

"Is this going to be very expensive?" I asked.

"Well, now," Tony said, and laughed. "But let's look

it over and see just exactly what you need. No sense getting something you don't *need*," he said jovially.

From then on, as nearly as I can remember, it was wheel alignment and something called camber or clamber or clabber, and wheel work was always expensive because every single car in the world except the make and model I owned had little adjustable pegs which could be fixed for next to nothing, but when Tony had to work with nonadjustable pegs, well, peg work was always expensive. Body work, too, would always set you back plenty, but it was the lives of my children I was taking in my hands if I let the fenders go.

"You got to regard this as an *investment*," Tony said earnestly. "Now, I wouldn't be treating you fair if I let those spark plugs go, for instance. You'd say I played you a pretty dirty trick if you had to come back a month from now for a big repair bill, you'd say to me, 'Tony, why didn't you fix those spark plugs a long time ago before I had to pay this big repair bill?' You see, it's an investment *now* so's it won't cost you so much *later*. Now take the muffler."

"Muffler," I said. Tony pointed to something under the car which I could not see.

"You see that?" he said. "I guess you didn't notice it before or you would of called it to my attention sooner. Lucky thing I saw it in time, I wasn't looking for anything like *that*."

"What would have happened?" I asked him nervously.

He shook his head. "Can't ever tell," he said. "*Nothing* might have happened—for a while. And then one day you're going up a hill, car full of children . . ." He shook his head again. "And the brake lining," he said. "*And* the ignition system."

I then made one of the bigger mistakes of my life. "How are the tires?" I asked.

Tony laughed. "You call those *tires?*" he demanded. "Why, let me tell you, one day I saw a guy, had his two little children with him, and I said to him—"

TWO WEEKS LATER I had my car back and we had managed to borrow enough extra money to pay the bill, upon which Tony had presumably retired to a little home in the hills to grow hollyhocks. The car looked and acted almost exactly the same except that the tank full of gas I had left in it was down almost to nothing. Tony said that was because they had to drive it in and out of the garage so many times.

I took everybody, including the dog, for a ride, and we went around the block four or five times, congratulating one another upon our new mobility. I discovered that my former usual attitude of timid acquiescence was not consistent with someone who could drive a car, so I fell gradually into a new personality, swashbuckling and brazen, with a cigarette usually hanging out of one corner of my mouth because I had to keep both hands on the wheel. We began to make plans for driving across the country to visit Grandma and Grandpa in California.

Some time later, while I, cigarette in the corner of my mouth, was stirring butterscotch pudding at the stove, and Laurie was glueing a model airplane at the kitchen table and Jannie was making double marshmallow chocolate ice cream pineapple coffee cake at *her* stove, Laurie raised his head and asked, "We've got a car now, haven't we?"

"We have," I said. "Why?"

"Why'd we get a car?" Laurie asked. "We never had one before."

"Daddy still walks for his haircut," Jannie said to her stove.

"That's because he's *scared* to get in the car," Laurie said.

"You know what I wish?" Jannie said. "I wish we had a airplane."

"Hey," Laurie said, interested. "*That* would be good. I could ride on the wing and Baby—"

"*I* could ride on the wing," Jannie said immediately. "I'm—"

"And what would *I* be doing?" I asked in a deadly voice.

They both turned and looked at me, their sweet trusting little faces confident.

At this time, Laurie was seven and a half, Jannie was four and a half, and Sally was one and a half. We had been in our big old house for four years, and space which had at one time seemed vast had contracted into little more than enough to hold us and the children and the cats and the dog. We had a car, and we had taken to telling one another that we couldn't imagine how we had ever got along without it. One of the left-hand pillars had begun to tremble during storms, and it was necessary to have it re-enforced.

It was when Jannie was very nearly five that the question of her name became desperately important. When she was born her father wanted to name her Jean and I wanted to name her Anne, and we compromised upon an arbitrary Joanne, although I frequently call her Anne and her father very often calls her Jean. Her brother calls her Honey, Sis, and Dopey, Sally calls her Nannie, and she calls herself, variously, Jean, Jane, Anne, Linda, Barbara, Estelle, Josephine, Geraldine, Sarah, Sally, Laura, Margaret, Marilyn, Susan, and–imposingly–Mrs. Ellenoy. The second Mrs. Ellenoy.

The *former* Mrs. Ellenoy–I have this straight from my daughter–was a lovely woman, mother of seven daughters, all named Martha, and she and Mr. Ellenoy used to be very angry with one another, until one day they grew so *very* angry that they up and killed each other with swords. As a result my daughter is the new Mrs. Ellenoy and has inherited all the Marthas as stepdaughters. When she is not named Jean, Linda, Barbara, Sally, and so on, but is being Mrs. Ellenoy, her daughters are allowed to assume these names, so that there is a constant bewildering shifting of names among them, and it is sometimes very difficult to remember whether you are addressing Janey Ellenoy or a small girl with seven daughters named Martha.

Since there is enough confusion in our house anyway, no one worries excessively about anyone else's name. Laurie has recently taken a flat stand on being called Laurie, and insists upon being addressed as either Laurence or Sir. Sally was named Sarah when she started, got shortened to Sally, and immediately got into trouble with Sally Ellenoy, so now we call the one Baby and the other Sallyellenoy. Baby is unmistakable, as is Dog for the dog, since *his* name is Toby and Baby renamed him Bowowby and Laurence renamed him Trigger and Mrs. Ellenoy generally calls him Child. The two cats look exactly alike, so we call them Kitty, generally. I myself use two names, a maiden name professionally and a married name, and my husband, who is addressed in all variants of father from Pappy to Da, now answers to almost anything, even—being a man not easily thrown off balance—Mr. Ellenoy.

In places where we have specific locations, such as our beds, or the dinner table, it is easy enough for us to address one another by facing the place we want. Equally, particular questions may be identified and caught by the person they most concern, so that something like "Did you know the bank called about that overdraft?" or "Didn't I tell you to change into a clean dress?" or "Do you want to go outside *again?*" or "Did she eat up all her nice cereal?" can easily be answered by the correct character, without all the trouble of trying to remember a name, or the rudeness of pointing. It is only on such a general question as "Well, who hasn't washed for dinner?" that the bitter matter of identification comes up.

I know what they all *look* like, of course. The dog has four feet and is far larger than the cats, who operate as a two-part unit anyway. The boy is dirty and wears a disgraceful pair of blue jeans. The father looks worried and a little bit overwhelmed. The older daughter is larger than the younger daughter, although there is an uncanny shifting of identity there, since the smaller wears the clothes the larger wore a short while before, and they both have blond curls and blue eyes. But as to trying to remember, for instance, which two out of three have already had chicken pox and which one was innoculated for whooping cough and whether any given one of them got all three prescribed injections or one of them got nine, and, worst, which of the Ellenoy girls got spanked for breaking Laurence's six-shooter and who told on her, I go all to pieces.

For example: I glanced out of the kitchen window one Sunday morning and found my older daughter up to her knees in a mud puddle. "Joanne," I said sharply, rapping on the glass in traditional manner with my wedding ring. She turned and smiled and I dried my hands on the dish towel and made for the back door. "What are you doing in that mud?"

My daughter looked at me, amused. "*This* is Mrs. Ellenoy," she said. "*I*'m over there." And she pointed.

One trouble about all this is that it is extraordinarily easy to be taken in by any particular statement.

"Joanne," I said, addressing the empty air where she was pointing, "get out of that mud puddle this minute."

"Get out at once," Mrs. Ellenoy added emphatically. "Joanne, I'm ashamed of you." She turned to me. "I don't know what we're going to do with her," she said. "Joanne," she added again, "you heard your mother. Get out of that mud puddle right now." She nodded reassuringly at me. "She'll be right in," she said. "I'll stay out here and wait for her."

I went back inside, talking to myself, and after a minute Mrs. Ellenoy poked her head in through the kitchen door. "Martha's out here," she said, "and she won't stop crying till you give her a cookie."

"I'm not giving a cookie to any little girl covered with mud," I said.

"*Martha*'s not covered with mud," Mrs. Ellenoy said reasonably. "That was bad Anne. Martha's been playing quietly under the apple tree all this time."

There was the frightful moment in the restaurant when all seven Ellenoy girls tried to climb onto Mrs. Ellenoy's lap just as the waitress was putting down a plate of soup. "You *can't* get into my lap now, can't you see I'm having my lunch?" Mrs. Ellenoy said crossly, and the waitress gave me a startled look and retreated, backing directly into Laurence's spurs. There was the black morning the census taker spent at our house, since she arrived before I was dressed and my daughter entertained her until I came down. There was the uncomfortable incident when my daughter trotted in to me and said, "There's a lady outside named Mrs. Harper and she wants to know will you give her a dollar?" and I replied absently, "Tell Mrs. Harper she may take the penny off my desk and not to bother me any more." My daughter told Mrs. Harper and Mrs. Harper went away furious and a little frightened, and I was entered on the P.-T.A. books as refusing to pay my dues.

Or there was this most touching incident which has really exposed my husband; as I say, he is a man not easily thrown off balance.

I glanced into the study the other morning and found my older daughter settling herself on the couch next to her father, who was reading the paper. She had *The Wizard of Oz* under her arm and as I passed by, smiling fondly, she asked her father, "Will you read for a minute to me?" In my subsequent wanderings through the house I frequently passed the study door and heard the comfortable drone of my husband's voice plowing his way toward the Emerald City. Finally, looking in and seeing him still reading aloud, but alone, I said in surprise, "Still reading?"

"I'm reading to Marilyn till Jean gets back," he said, not looking up from the book.

I went outdoors to where my daughter was sitting drawing pictures under the apple tree and said conversationally, "Dad's still reading to Marilyn."

"I know," said my daughter, nodding. "I got too restless so I left."

We played a game of croquet and picked some flowers for the house and ordered the groceries and my husband was still reading.

After a while my daughter went back into the study, said softly, "Move over, Marilyn," and settled down to hear the rest of the book.

"Dad was reading out loud to himself all morning," my son observed as he sat down at the dinner table that evening.

"No, I wasn't," said my husband. "I was reading to Marilyn."

"I thought you were reading to yourself," Laurie said.

"Marilyn doesn't brush her teeth," Mrs. Ellenoy said. "*None* of my girls brush their teeth," she added wistfully, "but all of them were dancing this afternoon. All the girls were dancing in the garden. There was Martha, and Sallyellenoy and Janey and Linda and Margaret—"

"You know what I wish?" Laurie demanded of his father. "I wish I was in Texas right now on a horse."

"—and Estelle and Barbara and Josephine and they were

all dancing," Mrs. Ellenoy continued. "And all us Ellenoys, we were dancing too."

"*Did* you call the bank?" my husband said, raising his voice to be heard.

"All dancing," said Mrs. Ellenoy happily, "all the girls were dancing."

"Mommy," said Sally, thumping crazily on her dish with her spoon, "Daddy, Nannie, Kitty, Mommy, Okay, Goodbye, cookie?"

Jannie sang softly, in a minor counterpoint, "Sally's bottom is dry as a fly, so goodbye, my peekaboo Sally."

Sally had consumed her chicken and her potatoes and was eating her peas one by one with her fingers, Jannie was daintily making designs in her potatoes with the back of her spoon, Laurie waved a chicken leg at his father and said vigorously, "say, *listen*, you know what's funny?" I was remembering the time the waitress backed into Laurie's spurs; sooner or later, I suppose, there must be in every mother's life the inevitable moment when she has to take two small children shopping in one big store. Although I keep telling myself that Laurie and Jannie are not more undisciplined, less poised, than any other two children of their age, I could not, for anything in the world, take them into public view again. Jannie had needed shoes, and Laurie some kind of trousers, made of any material on the order of sheet iron, to wear to school, where apparently the second-graders amuse themselves during the long weary days by cutting holes in one another's clothes with scissors. I felt, erroneously, that it was preferable to buy Jannie's shoes and Laurie's pants in a large department store in the nearest city, rather than relying so entirely upon our small local stores, and it seemed to me that I should have the children with me to try things on. I *have* tried buying shoes for children with an outline of the child's foot traced on paper, but it is never completely satisfactory, aside from the pleasure the child gets out of having his foot traced.

It was a Wednesday morning when I assembled the children, Laurie having been kept home from school because I had a faint idea that Wednesday was the day when the stores were least crowded. I have no idea what persuaded me that the stores were going to be least crowded on Wednesday, although, as it turned out, it hardly mattered, since my children proved to be able to assemble a crowd at any given time on any given day.

We all looked very nice when we started out. Jannie was wearing her best dark red coat, with high blue stockings and a blue beret. Laurie was wearing his suit, which was a little too small for him, his dark blue tie, his spurs, and two pearl-handled revolvers, although I took a firm stand on his not loading them with caps. I was wearing a gray fur coat and the low-heeled shoes which I ordinarily wear around the house, but which I chose to wear shopping this day because low heels seemed more practical for the broken field running I expected to be doing. I had also, with rare good sense, stripped for action in that I carried absolutely nothing—no pocketbook, no gloves, no hat. I assumed, and correctly, that I was going to need all the hands I could get. I had my money in a little purse in my pocket, which I kept feeling nervously to make sure it was still there. I had left simple instructions for my husband on care of Sally ("if she cries, ignore her, unless she seems to be crying because she's in trouble—you'll be sure to recognize the difference—or else she might be crying because she's dropped her little suitcase out of the crib and wants you to pick it up, but be *sure* not to let her have the doll in the blue dress because its arm is broken and if she wants a drink make her take the half-glass of milk in the left-hand lower corner of the refrigerator because that's what she left from breakfast and if she goes in the playpen—") and he had given each of the older children a dime.

We sailed off in fine style, as far as the front door, where Jannie flatly declined to move further unless allowed to take along her doll carriage and doll. There was a violent argument; I took the always-losing position of "Either the doll stays home or you do," and Laurie swung on the knob of the front door saying "Come *on*, let's *go*." We got the doll carriage into a bus, finally, and all the way into town Jannie bent over it, crooning to her doll about how no one was going to leave sweet dolly at home while Jannie had anything to say about it; Laurie shot people from the bus window with his pearl-handled revolvers. I made rapid and inaccurate mental calculations about the probable price of lunch and the cost of transporting the doll carriage in taxis. Fortunately, my shopping list was simple: J. shoes; L. pants, and if I *did* happen to be anywhere near a suit department I might take a look at dark suits, the simple kind they don't seem to make any more.

"Move over," Jannie said to me, "you're sitting on Linda."

"*Linda*'s not coming?" I said incredulously.

"Certainly she's coming," Jannie said, "and you're sitting on her."

"You and your old girls," Laurie said, drawing in his head and pointing his gun. "There, I shot her."

A crisis was averted at that moment because the bus stopped in front of the department store where I fondly believed they had shoes in Jannie's size and pants in Laurie's strength and suits in my shade of darkness. We got out of the bus, apologizing, and reached the sidewalk without trouble—quite an accomplishment, with the doll carriage, Linda, and Laurie, who remembered his manners at the last minute, and ran back from the sidewalk to hold the door for me after I had already gotten out, leaving Jannie alone and disconsolate, so that she started sadly down the street alone pushing her carriage, with the crowd separating to make a path for her, and one or two old ladies turning to smile and tell one another that she was sweet, and cute, and adorable.

By the time Laurie and I, shouting, had caught up, Jannie and the doll carriage were almost inextricably caught in a revolving door.

I think, every time I step into a department store with my children, surely, I think, it *is* possible to take children shopping, otherwise, the ten thousand mothers and children surrounding us at this moment are either figments of my imagination, which is perfectly possible, or else actors paid by the store to make itself look busy, which is also perfectly possible, but impractical considering the amount of trade I am likely to bring in with Laurie and Jannie; it *must* be, I keep telling myself, a simple and wholesome business, to buy one's children clothes. Doll carriage, revolvers, and all, we got onto the escalator, a machine which I am absolutely convinced is intent upon trapping small unwary feet or, preferably, well-shod maternal feet, and I said, "Careful, children, please."

"Watch your feet, Linda," Jannie said repeatedly as we went from the first to the second floor, "watch your feet, Marilyn. Susan, watch your *feet*."

I was carrying the doll carriage by then, under my arm; when I recognized the third, and boy's floor, I said briskly, "All right, we get off here." Doll carriage under my arm, I alighted and used my free hand to swing Jannie off the escalator. Laurie disembarked with a theatrical gesture which found me leaping backward to catch him before he went along with the escalator to whatever submerged and awful depths it departs; "What's the matter with *you?*" Laurie demanded irritably, "scared or something?"

"Linda," Jannie said anxiously, "watch your step getting off the escalator. Susan, be careful. Linda, jump now; Barbara, help Linda; Marilyn, wait for your turn; Margaret–"

"Jannie," I said, "please stop. They can get off by themselves." I was beginning to be aware of a familiar and dreadful feeling: that of being stared at by hordes of people–salesladies, floorwalkers, mothers, immaculate children, and perhaps truant officers. "Come on," I said nervously, and added just in time, "my dears."

I put the doll carriage down and Jannie settled herself behind it, hands on the bar, alert and ready to start. "Linda," she said softly, "all girls, get in line behind me, please."

"We going to get *clothes?*" Laurie demanded, looking about him with vast contempt. "I thought you said *lunch*."

"A pair of pants for you, dear," I said sweetly. I was tacking the "dear" onto every sentence I spoke for fear someone should hear me. At this moment, just as our procession was ready to get under way, a large, red-faced man in a rumpled brown suit accosted us. "Madam?" he said inquiringly to me.

He was not a floorwalker, he was certainly not a salesclerk; he might just possibly have been some cowboy hero in mufti–although in that case he would probably have addressed himself to my son, where he would be assured of at least some comprehension–and he was not, I discovered by feeling at my pocket, a thief. "This little boy buying clothes?" he asked me, gesturing grandly toward Laurie.

"He is," I said. "Aren't we, dear?" to Laurie.

"Well, Madam," the man went on, smiling alternately at me and—with some tentative geniality—at Laurie, "I represent the Real Western Rancho Clothes for Boys Company. We are meeting boys shopping here, talking to them and to their mothers, trying to find out what boys *really* like in clothes. For instance," he went on, obviously gaining courage as Laurie and I—not being notoriously quick thinkers—only stared blankly at him, "for instance, here is a boy, I can tell right away, who is lively and full of fun and a real Western Rancho type, right out there with the cowhands at chow time—" he squatted down by Laurie and looked Laurie straight in the eye,"—and this critter here *needs* real cowpunching duds. Why, I bet this hombre knows a good suit of clothes when he sees it, don't you pardner?" He gave Laurie's shoulder a friendly shake. "What's this?" he demanded, "your shooting iron?"

Laurie stepped back. "It's a gun," he said. "You think it was a squirrel or something?"

The man laughed commercially, and I said in warning, "Laurie," and added, "dear." "Bright boy," the man said to me. "Now, come along, pardner, and let this here coyote take your picture."

"Do what?" said Laurie.

The man laughed again, and tried to give Laurie a little tug over to where another, unhappy-looking man, this one in an ill-fitting cowboy hat, was standing behind a camera, looking as though he would have been more at ease sitting on a corral fence in front of a dry martini; "You're next, Pancho," the man in the brown suit said insistently to Laurie.

"Hey," Laurie said, holding back. I could tell that he had not yet decided upon his final attitude toward this, but I could have told the man a thing or two about getting a firm grip on a boy's arm (never *below* the elbow). Jannie, who had wandered off down the aisles, pushing her doll carriage and indicating to Linda, Marilyn, Susan, and the rest various interesting sights they passed, now turned and called to me from the other end of the store, "Mommy, Linda wants you to get her this cowboy hat."

"*Cut* it out," Laurie said, pulling away easily.

"That gun loaded?" said the man, grinning. "You aim to shoot, stranger?"

"What?" said Laurie.

The man looked up at me. "He have TV yet?" he asked.

"Yes," I said, "but–"

"Well, what we waiting for, fella?" said the man. "Put your picture in the paper," he said. "All the girls'll see it."

Laurie froze. "Girls?" he said. "What girls?"

"Don't you have a girl friend?" the man said.

"I'm a married man," Laurie said.

"*Laurie,*" I said.

"Mommy." The doll carriage smacked against the backs of my knees. "Mommy," Jannie said, "I called you and called you and Linda called you too and you didn't answer me. Who's that man talking to Laurie?"

She went over close to the man and stared curiously into his face. "Who're you?" she asked. "Does Mommy know you're talking to Laurie?"

"M'sister," Laurie said; perhaps it was the last shred of courtesy left in him, or perhaps he was just terribly afraid that this stranger might think Jannie a girl friend.

"Well," said the man, "and is this little sister? Do you pull her hair?" he asked Laurie.

"*My* hair?" said Jannie, and laughed shortly. "And this," she added, "is Linda, and this is Marilyn, and this is Susan, and this is Barbara, and this is—Margaret? Where is Margaret?"

"Margaret?" said the man in the brown suit.

"Margaret," Jannie said sharply. She stamped her foot. "Margaret," she said, "you come here at once. How dare you run away like that? You ought to be spanked right now and here. You bad, bad, bad, bad—"

"Jannie," I said helplessly, "please don't scold her. She's so little."

"The more reason she should stay with Linda," Jannie said.

The man in the brown suit, who had been steadily backing away, now rose to his feet and looked long at Laurie and long at Jannie and then, inscrutably, at me. As he turned away, Jannie said, "You can take *my* picture if you want to, and Linda's and Marilyn's and everybody's but Margaret."

A large lady accompanied by a young boy swept past me and grabbed the stranger by the arm. "You the man taking pictures in the paper?" she asked. "Look, you the man?"

"I always wear Western Rancho clothes," said the little boy anxiously; he was wearing a pale blue gabardine suit, with a darker blue shirt and a dark red figured tie, neatly knotted. His shoes were polished, his tie pin glittered. His nails, I could see, were clean, as were his ears. He was wearing a neat cap, which he took off when he addressed the man in the brown suit. I glanced at Laurie; he was staring with his mouth open.

"Hello, boy," Jannie said. She turned to Laurie. "Boy?" she whispered, "or girl?"

"Huh," said Laurie.

"Madam," said the man in the brown suit, "here is a boy, I can tell right away, who is lively and full of fun and a real Western Rancho type, right out there with—"

"In all the papers?" said the woman; she was removing a spot from the boy's face with the corner of her handkerchief.

"Look," said Laurie loudly, "he got dirty, poor thing."

With a certain obscure pride in my son I took him by the back of the collar and hauled him purposefully toward the department where they had pants in his size; I pushed the doll carriage with my other hand while Jannie shepherded Linda, Marilyn, and the rest, with loud, laughing directions. I was also carrying Jannie's beret and her coat —they could not be set on top of the carriage without disturbing sweet dolly—and Laurie's suit jacket, and my own coat. My voice was getting shrill, but I was still doggedly adding "dear" to every sentence.

Once I got Laurie into the department where I wanted him, there was small trouble in getting him to choose a pair of pants. He also chose a gabardine suit much like the one the boy with his picture in the paper had been wearing, priced at $59.95, a complete suit of space cadet armor, priced at $47.00, a very odd fur hat which for some reason he admired, and which would have cost me $7.50, a shaggy suede jacket which was called a Buffalo Bill jacket, and which was priced modestly at $32.50, pants to match $17.00. I one by one eliminated these articles, on the grounds that they were too heavy, too furry, too shaggy, or too expensive. I proffered a bright red bow tie, priced at sixty-nine cents, as a substitute. After some argument, during the course of which I told him he could buy anything he wanted with his father's dime, he was persuaded to take the bow tie or nothing, and the salesman remarked in an aside to me, "*I* don't think these fads will last." Jannie had amused herself during this time by trying on one fur hat after another, to the extreme bewilderment of Linda, Marilyn, and the rest. She also fell into conversation with a harmless old lady who was trying to find a birthday gift for her nephew and who had great difficulty resisting Jannie's invitation to come shopping with us and Mommy would buy her a pair of shoes.

I added the package with the bow tie and two pairs of corduroy pants to the doll carriage, Jannie's coat and beret, Laurie's suit jacket, and my own coat. Fortunately Jannie's shoes were on the same floor; we could not conceivably get into an elevator, and I was most reluctant to get back onto the escalator. In the shoe department, Jannie sat herself down, ranged her girls about her, and, folding her hands peaceably, announced that she intended to have a pair of shiny black shoes with high-heels and pretty straps and sparkles and no toes.

"Shoes for the kiddies?" said the shoe clerk brightly, setting his little stool down before us.

"Just me and my girls," Jannie said. "We all want shoes."

The clerk did not hear this because I was telling him loudly that we wanted something in a solid brown oxford with a good sole. I knew I was going to have to reach a compromise somewhere along this line, and I thought I would start from rock bottom and so, going up, have more bargaining power. When the clerk brought the brown oxford Jannie dismissed it after a brief glance. "That's for my brother," she said, "bring something for *me*."

During the excruciating process of Jannie's buying herself a pair of shoes, Laurie amused himself by counting the number of boxes the clerk brought out, Jannie held steadfastly to the high-heeled black sandal, and I grew very tense and began saying things like "How will you go to *school* without shoes because you are certainly *not* going to have any *shoes* until you start behaving like a little *lady* . . ."

We reached a tearful compromise on a pair of black patent leather shoes, completely impractical, but better, I reassured myself, than the black sandals with the high heels. Jannie remarked, as we left the shoe department, "I'm glad you're not my mommy. My mommy always buys me the shoes I want, and if *you* were my mommy I would run away."

"Those are the worst shoes I ever saw in all my life," Laurie told her.

"They're beautiful," said Jannie. "All my girls have shoes just like them."

I had added the package with the shoes to my other portage.

"Let's have *lunch*," Laurie said.

I looked at the clock with the faint unconscious hope common to all mothers that time will somehow have passed magically away and the next time you look it will be bed-time. It was ten minutes to twelve; a good eight hours to go before the nightly miracle, but a legitimate time for lunch.

"Well, children," I said, smiling sweetly and falsely around the table in the restaurant, "well, now we're going to remember our company manners, aren't we?"

Jannie looked bright and alert, and said sweetly, "Can we have two desserts?"

"Perhaps, dears," I said with that same sweet smile, "if we eat allllll our lunch."

Waitresses always take a very long time when you are waiting at a restaurant table with children. I would prefer not to believe that this is due entirely to the general appearance and deportment of my children at the table. At any rate, we had been sitting–me with my hands neatly folded, Laurie with his elbows on the table, and Jannie sliding down in her chair so that her chin rested comfortably on the edge of the table–waiting, I say, for perhaps ten minutes, while waitresses scurried busily past, serving the tables on either side of us, bringing extra pats of butter, stopping to chat merrily, hovering solicitously over customers who could not make up their minds.

"When is she going to *come?*" Laurie demanded.

"I want my lunch," Jannie amplified. She reached out and gave a sharp slap against one of Laurie's elbows, so that his head crashed down and his chin cracked on the table. "Keep your elbows off the table," she said admonishingly.

"Now, children," I said in my gentle voice, scowling fiercely at Jannie, "now, children, remember we intended to use our very best manners."

"Well, *she*–" Laurie began righteously.

"He had his elbows on the table," Jannie said. "Mommy dearest, Laurie was putting his old elbows on the table, Mommy dear."

"*Listen,*" Laurie said, "*she* went and–"

"Darlings," I said, my voice more sugary, if possible, than

before, "let us remember that *other* people are trying to eat *their* lunches, too, and we–"

"What?" Laurie said to Jannie, who was whispering earnestly in his direction.

"Nothing," Jannie said, looking attentively at me. "We *are* being good children, Mommy dearest. We *are* letting other people eat their lunch."

"That's right, dear," I said to her, "*my* children are such good–"

"Why are you talking funny like that?" Laurie asked me, interested, just as the waitress showed up beside us. "You sound like a cat."

He and Jannie both began to laugh loudly. "She sounds like a cat," Jannie told the waitress.

"You wanna order?" the waitress said to me.

"I want spaghetti," Jannie said immediately.

"*I* want spaghetti," Laurie said.

"Let me see." I consulted the menu. "Omelette?" I said to Laurie. And, to Jannie, "Vegetable plate?"

"No," Jannie said, "spaghetti."

"No spaghetti today," the waitress said. She sighed deeply, fussing with her hair. "Ony what's onna menu," she said.

"Chicken salad?" I said. "Liver?"

"Liver," Laurie said, and made a noisy gesture of distaste. "Liver-biver-shiver-tiver-wiver-niver–"

"Liver-liver-liver," said Jannie.

"Children," I said, recollecting myself in time, so that

it came out gentle. "We must *not* take up all this time deciding."

"I decided," Laurie said. "Spaghetti."

Jannie switched sides abruptly. "Vegetable plate," she said. "Mommy dear."

"Justa minute," the waitress said, and departed.

Two unpleasant-looking women wearing flowered hats got up ostentatiously from the next table and moved to a table across the room. "Look here," I said, my voice just loud enough to carry across our own table, "one more word out of either of you and *you*–" eyeing Laurie "–will find yourself being spanked right here in public where everyone will laugh at you and *you*–" eyeing Jannie "–will find yourself being spanked somewhere in private where *no* one can hear you. And right now Jannie is going to have a vegetable plate for lunch and Laurie is going to have a chicken salad and I am going to have spaghetti–I mean, a club sandwich. Now does anyone have anything to say?"

They stared at me numbly. Laurie scowled, and showed his teeth, and was quiet. Jannie's face moved, the corners of her mouth turned down, her great blue eyes filled with tears, and she took a deep breath. "Just one howl out of you," I said sweetly, "and all your girls get shut outdoors tonight." She closed her mouth, and blinked.

Laurie made a move as though to reach for his gun. "That man can still take your picture, you know," I said. He put both hands back on the table.

"Ha, ha," Jannie said bitterly to me, "*you*'ve only got one head."

"Put your foot in here," Laurie told me, extending his water glass.

The waitress reappeared. "Kids made up their minds?" she said.

"Vegetable plate," said Jannie meekly.

"Chicken salad," Laurie said politely. "And two cups of coffee, please."

"Two glasses of milk," I told her. "And I will have a club sandwich."

"And Linda will have spaghetti," Jannie said, "and Marilyn will have spaghetti, and Susan will have spaghetti . . ."

"Jannie," I said sharply.

"And Margaret," Jannie whispered, "Margaret has to have the vegetable plate."

If I gave up any idea of my dark suit, all we still had to do was manage the escalator going down and get ourselves into a bus and out again at home. I sighed. "I wonder how Daddy and Sally are getting along," I said.

It was at that moment that the waitress approached our table with the plate of soup and the seven little Ellenoys backed her into those spurs.

WE ARE ALL of us, in our family, very fond of puzzles. I do double-crostics and read mystery stories, my husband does baseball box scores and figures out batting averages, and says he knows the odds against drawing a fourth ace, Laurie is addicted to the kind of puzzle which begins "There are fifty-four items in this picture beginning with the letter C," Jannie does children's jigsaws, and Sally can put together an intricate little arrangement of rings and bars which has had the rest of us stopped for two months. We are none of us, however, capable of solving the puzzles we work up for ourselves in the oddly diffuse patterns of our several lives, and along with such family brain-teasers as "Why is there a pair of rollerskates in Mommy's desk?" and "What is *really* in the back of Laurie's closet?" and "Why doesn't Daddy wear the nice shirts Jannie picked out for Father's Day?" we are all of us still wondering nervously about what might be called the Great Grippe Mystery. As a matter of fact, I should be extremely grateful if anyone could solve it for us, because we are certainly very short of blankets, and it is annoying not to have *any* kind of an answer. Here, in rough outline, is our puzzle:

Our house is, as I have said, large, and the second floor has four bedrooms and a bathroom, all opening out onto a long narrow hall which we have made even narrower by lining it with bookcases so that every inch of hall which is not doorway is books. As is the case with most houses, both the front door and the back door are downstairs on the first floor. The front bedroom, which is my husband's and mine, is the largest and lightest, and has a double bed.

The room next down the hall belongs to the girls, and contains a crib and a single, short bed. Laurie's room, across the hall, has a double-decker bed and he sleeps on the top half. The guest room, at the end of the hall, has a double bed. The double bed in our room is made up with white sheets and cases, the baby's crib has pink linen, and Jannie's bed has yellow. Laurie's bed has green linen, and the guest room has blue. The bottom half of Laurie's bed is never made up, unless company is going to use it immediately, because the dog traditionally spends a large part of his time there and regards it as his bed. There is no bed table on the distaff side of the double bed in our room. One side of the bed in the guest room is pushed against the wall. No one can fit into the baby's crib except the baby; the ladder to the top half of Laurie's double-decker is very shaky and stands in a corner of the room; the children reach the top half of the bed by climbing up over the footboard. All three of the children are accustomed to having a glass of apple juice, to which they are addicted, by their bedsides at night. Laurie uses a green glass, Jannie uses a red glass, Sally uses one of those little flowered cheese glasses, and my husband uses an aluminum tumbler because he has broken so many ordinary glasses trying to find them in the dark.

I do not take cough drops or cough medicine in any form.

The baby customarily sleeps with half a dozen cloth books, an armless doll, and a small cardboard suitcase which holds the remnants of half a dozen decks of cards. Jannie is very partial to a pink baby blanket, which has shrunk from many washings. The girls' room is very warm, the guest room moderately so; our room is chilly, and Laurie's room is quite cold. We are all of us, including the dog, notoriously easy and heavy sleepers; my husband never eats coffee cake.

My husband caught the grippe first, on a Friday, and snarled and shivered and complained until I prevailed upon him to go to bed. By Friday night both Laurie and Sally were feverish, and on Saturday Jannie and I began to cough and sniffle. In our family we take ill in different manners; my husband is extremely annoyed at the whole procedure and is convinced that his being sick is somebody's fault, Laurie tends to become a little light-headed and strew handkerchiefs around his room, Jannie coughs and coughs and coughs, Sally turns bright red, and I suffer in stoical silence, so long as everyone knows clearly that I am sick. We are each of us privately convinced that our own ailment is far more severe than anyone else's. At any rate, on Saturday night I put all the children into their beds, gave each of them half an aspirin and the usual fruit juice, covered them warmly, and then settled my husband down for the night with his tumbler of water and his cigarettes and matches and ashtray; he had decided to sleep in the guest room because it was warmer. At about ten o'clock I checked to see that all the children were covered and asleep and that Toby was in his place on the bottom half of the double-decker. I then took two sleeping pills and went to sleep in my own bed in my own room. Because my husband was in the guest room I slept on his side of the bed, next to the bed table. I put my cigarettes and matches on the end table next to the ashtray, along with a small glass of brandy, which I find more efficacious than cough medicine.

I woke up some time later to find Jannie standing beside the bed. "Can't sleep," she said. "Want to come in *your* bed."

"Come along," I said. "Bring your own pillow."

She went and got her pillow and her small pink blanket and her glass of fruit juice, which she put on the floor next to the bed, since she had got the side without any end table. She put her pillow down, rolled herself in her pink blanket, and fell asleep. I went back to sleep, but sometime later Sally came in, asking sleepily, "Where's Jannie?"

"She's here," I said. "Are you coming in bed with us."

"Yes," said Sally.

"Go and get your pillow, then," I said.

She returned with her pillow, her books, her doll, her suitcase, and her fruit juice, which she put on the floor next to Jannie's. Then she crowded in comfortably next to Jannie and fell asleep. Eventually the pressure of the two of them began to force me uneasily toward the edge of the bed, so I rolled out wearily, took my pillow and my small glass of brandy and my cigarettes and matches and my ashtray and went into the guest room, where my husband was asleep. I pushed at him and he snarled, but he finally moved over to the side next to the wall, and I put my cigarettes and matches and my brandy and my ashtray on the end table next to *his* cigarettes and matches and ashtray and tumbler of water and put my pillow on the bed and fell asleep. Shortly after this he woke me and asked me to let him get out of the bed, since it was too hot in that room to sleep and he was going back to his own bed. He took his pillow and his cigarettes and matches and his ashtray and his aluminum glass of water and went padding off down the hall. In a few minutes Laurie came into the guest room where I had just fallen asleep again; he was carrying his pillow and his glass of fruit juice. "Too cold in my room," he said, and I moved out of the way and let him get into the bed on the side next to the wall. After a few minutes the dog came in, whining nervously, and came up onto the bed and curled himself up around Laurie and I had to get out or be smothered. I gathered together what of my possessions I could, and made my way into my own room, where my husband was asleep with Jannie on one side and the baby on the other. Jannie woke up when I came in and said, "Own bed," so I helped her carry her pillow and her fruit juice and her pink blanket back to her own bed.

The minute Jannie got out of our bed the baby rolled over and turned sideways, so there was no room for me. I could not get into the crib and I could not climb into the top half of the double-decker, so since the dog was in the guest room I went and took the blanket off the crib and got into the bottom half of the double-decker, setting my brandy and my cigarettes and matches and my ashtray on the floor next to the bed. Shortly after that Jannie, who apparently felt left out, came in with her pillow and her pink blanket and her fruit juice and got up into the top half of the double-decker, leaving her fruit juice on the floor next to my brandy.

At about six in the morning the dog wanted to get out, or else he wanted his bed back, because he came and stood next to me and howled. I got up and went downstairs, sneezing, and let him out, and then decided that since it had been so cold anyway in the bottom half of the double-decker I might as well stay downstairs and heat up some coffee and have that much warmth, at least. While I was waiting for the coffee to heat Jannie came to the top of the stairs and asked if I would bring *her* something hot, and I heard Laurie stirring in the guest room, so I heated some milk and put it into a jug and decided that while I was at it I might just as well give everybody something hot so I set out enough cups for everyone and brought out a coffee cake and put it on the tray and added some onion rolls for my husband, who does not eat coffee cake. When I brought the tray upstairs Laurie and Jannie were both in the guest room, giggling, so I set the tray down in there and heard Sally talking from our room in the front. I went to get her and she was sitting up in the bed talking to her father, who was only very slightly awake. "Play card?"

she was asking brightly, and she opened her suitcase and dealt him, onto the pillow next to his nose, four diamonds to the ace jack and the seven of clubs.

I asked my husband if he would like some coffee, and he said it was terribly cold. I suggested that he come down into the guest room, where it was warmer. He and the baby followed me down to the guest room, and my husband and Laurie got into the bed and the rest of us sat on the foot of the bed and I poured the coffee and the hot milk and gave the children coffee cake and my husband the onion rolls. Jannie decided to take her milk and coffee cake back into her own bed, and since she had mislaid her pillow she took one from the guest room bed. Sally of course followed her, going first back into our room to pick up *her* pillow. My husband fell asleep again while I was pouring his coffee, and Laurie set his hot milk precariously on the headboard of the bed and asked me to get his pillow from wherever it was, so I went into the double-decker and got him the pillow from the top, which turned out to be Jannie's, and her pink blanket was with it. I took my coffee cake and my coffee into my own bed and had just settled down when Laurie came in to say cloudily that Daddy had kicked him out of bed and could he stay in here. I said of course and he said he would get a pillow and he came back in a minute with the one from the bottom half of the double-decker which was mine. He went to sleep right away, and then the baby came in to get her books and her suitcase and decided to stay with her milk and her coffee cake, so I left and went into the guest room and made my husband move over and sat *there* and had my coffee. Meanwhile Jannie had moved into the top half of the double-decker, looking for her pillow, and had taken instead the pillow from Sally's bed and my glass of brandy and had settled down there to listen to Laurie's radio. I went downstairs to let the dog in and he came upstairs and got into his bed on the bottom half of the double-decker, and while I was gone my husband had moved back over onto the accessible side of the guest room bed so I went into Jannie's bed, which is rather too short, and I brought a pillow from the guest room, and my coffee.

At about nine o'clock the Sunday papers came and I went down to get them, and at about nine-thirty everyone woke up. My husband had moved back into his own bed when Laurie and Sally vacated it for their own beds, Laurie driving Jannie into the guest room when he took back the top half of the double-decker, and my husband woke up at ninc-thirty and found himself wrapped in Jannie's pink blanket, sleeping on Laurie's green pillow and with a piece of coffee cake and Sally's fruit juice glass, not to mention the four diamonds to the ace jack and the seven of clubs. Laurie, in the top half of the double-decker, had my glass of brandy and my cigarettes and matches and the baby's pink pillow. The dog had my white pillow and my ashtray. Jannie in the guest room had one white pillow and one blue pillow and two glasses of fruit juice and my husband's cigarettes and matches and ashtray and

Laurie's hot milk, besides her own hot milk and coffee cake and her father's onion rolls. The baby in her crib had her father's aluminum tumbler of water and her suitcase and books and doll and a blue pillow from the guest room, but no blanket.

The puzzle is, of course, what became of the blanket from Sally's bed? I took it off her crib and put it on the bottom half of the double-decker, but the dog did not have it when he woke up, and neither did any of the other beds. It was a blue-patterned patchwork quilt, and has not been seen since, and I would most particularly like to know where it got to. As I say, we are very short of blankets.

WITH COLDER WEATHER setting in, and school once more in sight, I took out the somewhat worn pair of red overalls which had had "Laurie" embroidered on them and crossed out, and "Jannie" embroidered underneath; I now crossed out the "Jannie" and embroidered "Sally" on them. They were a little thin in the seat, and the bottoms of the legs were frayed, but the sentiment was there. Sally also inherited hundreds of pullover shirts and thousands of unmatched socks. Laurie got a leather jacket, Jannie took to carrying a pocketbook, Ninki's third litter of kittens turned out to include one without a tail, and the family of a friend of Jannie's eagerly seized upon this one as a particularly delightful pet. Jannie entered a kind of private kindergarten, which consisted entirely of little girls and which met mornings in the home of a retired grade-school teacher; Jannie began to skip instead of walk and giggled unendurably with her friends. By the end of the first two weeks of school the mother of Jannie's friend called up indignantly to tell me that the kitten had suddenly begun to grow a tail, had grown half a tail and stopped, and that they now had a kitten with a half-tail, which they did not regard as a particularly delightful pet, and she strongly implied that we had deliberately misled them into believing that they were getting a kitten which would be permanently without a tail.

Sally at this time gave up any notion of being a co-operative member of a family, named herself "Tiger" and settled down to an unceasing, and seemingly endless, war against clothes, toothbrushes, all green vegetables, and bed. Her main weapon was chewing gum, which she stole out of Laurie's pockets and with which she could perform miracles of construction on her own hair, books, and, once, her father's typewriter.

I estimated that since we had moved into this house I had used up more than five hundred packages of chocolate pudding. A new school bus was proposed, to be put into service the next school year; the younger Harvey boy, who had been in high school when we moved into town, was to be the driver. Most reluctantly, with a great deal of hesitation and judicious packing and unpacking, and some vast confusion with white shirts, my husband made ready for a major trip to New York.

It was a solemn parting at the station; our two older children stood close to us, and Sally sat, rocking, on a luggage cart. Laurie had said "Where's the *train?*" four times, and Sally had indicated seven times that she planned to accompany her father. My husband had said perhaps eleven times that he was sure everything would be all right while he was gone, and I cannot remember how many times I must have said that he was not to worry about *us;* we would be fine. The train was fifteen minutes late, which gave us all time to repeat ourselves, and to make various other completely reasonable remarks like "Boy, I bet *you* wouldn't stand on those tracks when the train comes," (Laurie, to Jannie) and "Are you sure you packed those warm socks?" (me, to my husband) and "Suppose the train doesn't *ever* come?" (Jannie, to her father.)

"Old Mother Hubbid went to the cubbid," Sally said loudly and insistently.

"Boy," Laurie said to his father, "I sure wish that *train* would come. Let's go home," he said to me abruptly, "*he* can get on a train by hisself."

There was a general nervous stirring among the people on the platform; I had begun a stern remark to Laurie about how we had come here to say goodbye to Daddy, after all, but everyone began to say "Here it comes, here it comes," and Sally bounced up and down, shouting, and Jannie and Laurie both moved forward so that I had to grab quickly for the backs of their jackets. "Well," my husband said to me.

"Goodbye, goodbye," I said. My husband, running, turned and waved. The children all waved back enthusiastically and called "Goodbye, goodbye," and I hung on to the backs of their jackets. Sternly repressing a pang of honest envy, I watched the train move off and my husband waving at the window. "Well, children," I said at last, "home we go."

"Has Daddy gone?" Sally asked.

"All gone," Laurie said.

I shepherded them into the car, prevented Sally from climbing right on out the window on the other side, and began to pull on my gloves. "Old Mother Hubbid," Sally said, "went–"

"Hubbid, hubbid, hubbid," Laurie said. "What's so special about Mother Hubbid?"

"*I* was talking," Sally said with dignity. "Old–"

"Can't you ever talk about anything else in the *world?*"

"Can we have a popsicle?" Jannie asked, hanging over the back seat behind my head, "because Daddy's gone away, can we have a popsicle or a piece of bubble gum or a lollipop or a frozen custard or a popsicle? Because Daddy's gone away?"

"We're going directly home for dinner," I said. "Chocolate pudding for dessert."

"No chocolate pudding for *Dad,*" Laurie said mournfully.

In honor of Daddy's departure we also had hot dogs and baked beans; I fed the children first and then, fighting down as unworthy the thought of my husband dining, no doubt, on roast beef and caviar in that haunt of iniquity and high living, the railroad dining car, I had my dinner on a tray, eating my hot dog absent-mindedly and reading a mystery story. The house was very quiet after the children were asleep, and I remembered suddenly, without at all wanting to, that our nearest neighbors had gone to Florida for the winter. I went to bed early, taking along my mystery story and the cat, and fell asleep with the light on. Several times during the night I awoke nervously, because the cat was restless, and although it was uncomfortable sleeping with the light on, I was reluctant to turn it off; there was a distinct ominous creaking in the hall just outside my door and I was growing increasingly positive that I smelled smoke. At any rate, I woke up in the morning cross and uncooperative, to find that it was seven-thirty instead of seven (had that ominous creaking been the alarm I had forgotten to set?) and that what looked and sounded like rain outside the window was, actually, rain. I leaped out of bed, slammed the window shut, turned off the light, opened the door and yelled, "Isn't anybody *up?*" There was a swift, answering disturbance, as of several children hastily dropping coloring books and crayons, and moving purposefully toward school clothes. My teeth not brushed (first things first, I kept telling myself), I hurried to the kitchen, set water on to boil for oatmeal, filled the fruit juice glasses, and—first things first—plugged in the coffee pot. By the time Jannie reached the kitchen I had the bowls and spoons out; I gave her a quick appraising glance and said, "Take off that necklace. Those are your best shoes and it's raining. Put on a sweater instead of that blouse. Brush your teeth." And, beyond her to Sally, "Shoes on wrong feet. And I put out a pair of decent overalls for you last night, not a sunsuit. And you've got to wear socks." I put back my head and shouted, "Laurie!"

After a minute he called back "I'm getting dressed."

"Sally," I said, "go and wake your brother."

"It's cold," Jannie said. She shivered elaborately. "It's *terribly* cold."

"If you had on a sweater instead of a silk blouse—" I said. "Sally, wake your *brother*."

"I'm *cold*," Sally said.

"Awake," Laurie said, appearing in the kitchen doorway in his pajamas. "Hey, it's cold."

It began to occur to me that it *was* cold; I had been moving so fast up to now that I had not noticed the faint undefinable chill on everything I touched—the spoons, the cereal box, the backs of the chairs. I looked at Laurie, and Laurie looked at me, and then he said, nodding, "Yup. I sure bet it is."

I went into the living room, Laurie following me, Jannie following him, and Sally padding on behind, murmuring, "To get her poor doggie something to eat." The thermostat in the living room was set at seventy-two, the thermometer below it read sixty-one. I looked at Laurie again and he nodded reassuringly. Gingerly I turned the thermostate up to seventy-five, to eighty, and, not breathing, we all listened. There was no answering roar from the cellar; the furnace was off.

I am not of a mechanical turn of mind. I am wholeheartedly afraid of fuses and motorcycles and floor plugs and lightning rods and electric drills and large animals and most particularly of furnaces. Laboriously, over the space of years of married life, my husband has taught me to use such hazardous appliances as a toaster and an electric coffee pot, but no one is ever going to get me to go down cellar and fool around with a furnace. I had a fairly clear notion that the best way to get the house warm again was to march firmly to a little door in the monster's side and press the third little button from the left; my husband and the furnace man, working together, had once shown this to me, their voices rising shrilly as they explained it over and over; *no* furnace, my husband had said, touching his forehead with the tips of his fingers, has ever exploded because some woman pressed the third little button from the left, *no* furnace. "Lady," the furnace man had said, twisting his hands together, "suppose some day you *got* to start the furnace, and no one's around, say, and you *got* to start it—"

Rising to heights of heroism far beyond my usual abilities, I strode responsibly to the cellar door, the children crowding along behind me. "The furnace seems to be off," I said to Laurie. "I'll just run down and start it up again."

"Yeah," Laurie said. "You go right on down" He regarded me without optimism.

I set my hand on the cellar doorknob. "But something might be broken," I said. (Was it the *third* little button from the left? The second? The right?) "I don't want to turn it on if it's broken," I said to Laurie. "I wouldn't like to do it any damage."

"It might be out of gas," Jannie suggested.

I turned to her gratefully. "That's right," I said. "Now I think of it, it would be very dangerous to turn it on if there's no oil. It grinds the parts together," I told Laurie, who nodded gravely. "I better call the man," I said.

Anyway, we were quite late. *Very* late, as a matter of fact; it was eight-thirty before I had gotten all the shoes tied, all the oatmeal consumed, the hair combed, the teeth brushed, the lunch boxes filled, the homework collected, the jackets on, the rubbers located, and had sneaked in a cup of coffee for myself. I lined the children out into the car, checking like an electric eye for handkerchiefs and contraband, and succeeded in rooting out and confiscating a small plastic telephone and two pieces of bubble gum from Sally and a large ring set with a glittering ruby from Jannie. I shut the car door behind them, raced around to the other side to catch Sally going out the opposite window, counted again to make sure I had three of them, and sat down in the driver's seat with a little sigh.

"If you got *up* earlier," Jannie said critically, "we wouldn't have to hurry so."

I opened my mouth to answer, reflected in time that the poor dears were at present fatherless, and said with great moderation, "Well, at least we're in plenty of time *now*." I pressed the starter.

Jannie giggled. "In Laurie's school he sits with the girls because he's so *pretty*."

"*Hey*, now, you–"

"Children," I said, "do be still." I pressed the starter. "After all," I said, with a light little laugh, "Jannie only teases Laurie because she knows he minds it; suppose *you* try keeping your temper, Laurie, and see how quickly she–" I pressed the starter.

"Old Mother *Hubbid*," Sally swept into the silence, "*she* went to the cubbid to get her dog something to eat, and when *she* started to get breakfast *she* had oatmeal." She began to laugh wildly. "Oatmeal," she repeated helplessly, "oatmeal."

I pressed the starter and pulled out the choke.

"Won't the star cart?" Jannie asked. Laurie began to shriek with laughter and after a bewildered minute Jannie joined in. "Old Mother *Hubbid*–" Sally began.

I pressed the starter and pulled out the choke and began to bang both hands on the steering wheel.

"Why don't you get out and crank it?" Laurie asked, howling.

"Why don't you get yourself a horse or something?" Jannie asked.

"Old Mother–"

"Just flooded it," I said, my voice level and restrained and even faintly amused. "Silly old car," I said affectionately, and gave a vicious kick at the clutch.

"Hey," Laurie said, suddenly no longer entertained, "we gonna be *late?*"

"Certainly not. Just tell the teacher that the car–"

"I told her that the *last* time," Laurie said. His voice became panicky. "And she said," he went on, "if I'm not in my sneakers by quarter of nine they'll get a substitute at left tackle and–"

"*Why* won't it start?" Jannie asked insistently. "What's the matter with the car?"

Fatherless or not, I raised my voice. "Never *mind*," I said. I have been patient with my car through many of its moods, and there is little that we do not know about each other by now, the car and I. It knows perfectly, for instance, that I am made extremely nervous by a kind of low moaning sound it makes when it is unhappy, and I know clearly that if it has come into my car's obscure mind not to start, no siren's tricks of mine can make it. "Sell the filthy thing for fifty cents," I said nastily, and climbed out and went into the house, mumbling to myself, and dialed our village taxi.

"Again?" Mr. Williams said when I told him. "You figure it's the battery again?"

"The children," I said, "have just seven minutes to get to school."

"Well, they won't make it," he said. "Time I get up there and back again. But I figure it ain't going to shock the teachers none, them being late again." He giggled, and I hung up.

I saw Laurie and Jannie off to school in the taxi, stowing away lunch boxes and books, and cautioning Jannie firmly against getting out at the graded school instead of her kindergarten; I asked Mr. Williams to pick Jannie up at twelve and Laurie at three, and said I would pay him later, it being nearly nine o'clock by now. Then–first things first–I came back into the house and shut Sally into her room with her blocks and took up the telephone; since my teeth were chattering I called first of all the number of K. B. Anderson, Plumbing and Heating, and got Mrs. Anderson, who answered the phone mornings in the office. I told her who I was, and all about how our furnace had gone out, and asked could Mr. Anderson please come right over?

"Well," she said, "not *this* morning. He won't be back till dinner-time and then this afternoon he's got to put in a heater over to Sawyer's. Tomorrow, maybe."

"But we have no heat and the children–"

"Maybe not even tomorrow, though, now I think of it," she went on. "On account of that plumber's convention up to Waterville tonight. And you know what *they* are."

I agreed with haste that I did indeed know what they

were, and said anxiously that it was getting colder here, and the children–

"Whyn't you try young Dick Sampson over on Bridge Street?" she asked. "*He* used to do some plumbing afore he was married."

"Sampson?"

"No, it's not Bridge Street at all. I don't know what made me think it *was*. He *used* to be on Bridge Street, but then he took over that television repair service."

"So he won't be going to the plumber's convention?" I asked politely.

"Not *him*," she said with satisfaction. "He married one of the Wiley girls, *that's* why I thought first of Bridge Street. Mildred, I'd say it was."

"But the furnace–"

"East Main," she said. "Knew it would come to me. Or you might even try to get ahold of Bill England. There's one might know what to do, or any of the Hope boys."

"Thanks very much," I said. As I hung up, staring hopelessly at the names I had jotted down (I knew the Hope boys, and I would as soon have frozen to death) it occurred to me that among all the friends I had in town I might locate one with a husband who was not afraid to go down into our cellar and look at our furnace. Nancy, I thought; she and Cliff had once come over and helped us put down a rug. I dialed Nancy and she answered and I asked her how she was and she asked me how *I* was and I told her about my husband's being out of town and she told me about the new chairs they were getting for the porch and I said how I had meant to call her and she said it had been so long since we got together and I said we must have a bridge game sometime next week and she said she would call me and I said I'd get in touch with her and I was just about to hang up when I remembered and said oh, look, there was something I meant to ask her. So I told her the furnace was off and I didn't know how to start it and she said why didn't I call Anderson?

"There's a plumber's convention," I said.

"Again? But when William dropped the hairbrush down the drain and I called Anderson, Mrs. Anderson said there was a plumber's convention *then.* And that was only about six weeks ago because my mother–"

"But do you think that Cliff–?"

"He'd love to," she assured me. "I'll send him over just as soon as he gets home. He'll be *glad* to do it."

We decided we would certainly get in touch with one another very soon, and hung up. I called Eddie at the garage and asked him to come and get my car again, and he sighed and said did I think it was still going to be the fan belt this time? I washed the breakfast dishes and made the beds, and it occurred to me that when Eddie came for the car I might ask *him* to go down cellar and start the furnace, him being a mechanic and all, but when he finally did come for the car, I was on the phone; Nancy had called back to say she was sorry, it wasn't a plumber's convention, it was an oil burner convention, and she had done Mr. Anderson an injustice. So we agreed that we would have a bridge game real soon, and by that time Eddie had disappeared with my car. At lunchtime the taxi brought Jannie home from school and I recalled with abrupt clarity that I had meant to stop on my way that morning and pick up a loaf of bread. I gave Jannie and Sally crackers and peanut butter for lunch, and while they were murmuring sadly in the kitchen I went to the phone and called my friend Carol. She asked how I was and I asked how she was and she told me about the bad cold her boy had been having and I told her about my husband's being out of town and she said we must get together some evening soon. I said I would call her, and meanwhile would she mind picking up a loaf of bread for me when she went down to the store? Because something had gone wrong with my car. She said sympathetically that you certainly needed a car out on our road, didn't you, and did I mind being alone in our big house at night? I said no, oh, no, I was never nervous, and could she also get me a can of tunafish? I felt urgently that there was something I had forgotten, but had no time to stop and think because she was saying was there anything else? It was no trouble at all. So I told her that would be plenty, thanks, and it was so nice of her, and we must surely get together some time real soon.

I put Sally to bed for her nap, settled Jannie with puzzles and books to rest in Laurie's room, made myself some crackers and peanut butter, and sat down again with my mystery story. About two o'clock the small persistent nagging which had stayed with me since I spoke to Carol suddenly resolved itself when I discovered that the motive for the murder in my book had been a large inheritance. Money, I thought. Hadn't my husband given me a check to cash this morning?

The check was in my pocketbook, along with three quarters and a penny. Although Carol would hardly press me for the price of a loaf of bread and a can of tunafish, today was Tuesday and the laundryman was due. The check was surely too large for him to cash, but if I let the laundry bill go for a week, there was Mr. Williams to be paid for the taxis. If I told Mr. Williams I would pay him tomorrow, I could pay Carol for the loaf of bread and the can of tunafish. But tomorrow was Wednesday and that meant that before school Laurie and Jannie would each need thirty-five cents for milk money and my mind stopped dully before the problem of dividing three quarters into two thirty-five-centses. I was debating shelving the whole matter and going back to bed when there was a knock at the back door, and when I opened it, there was Mr. Anderson. "Missus said I should come right over," he explained. "Said you had no heat for the kids."

"The furnace is off," I said, to clarify the situation. "It's down cellar." Mr. Anderson—perhaps because of his pressing social obligations—operates always on a strictly cash basis; there is a rumor about him, implicitly believed by me, that if he is not paid immediately he goes right back downstairs and breaks the furnace again. "I hope you can fix it," I said weakly as Mr. Anderson disappeared down the cellar stairs, conversing cheerily as he went; by the time he had begun a sort of rhythmic banging on the boiler I was in Laurie's room, my back carefully turned to Jannie, examining his wallet, which contained eleven cents—not even enough to solve the milk money problem. I had been hoping for the five dollars his grandparents had sent him for a football, and would have kicked myself when I remembered that I had personally driven him into town so he could spend it on model cars. His bank, however, was on the dresser.

"What you doing?" Jannie asked from the bed. She put down a piece of puzzle to watch me.

"Looking for something," I said truthfully.

"Oh," Jannie said. "Is it there?"

"Yep," I said.

By the time Mr. Anderson came stamping back upstairs I was sitting cheerfully at the dining room table, running my fingers richly through a heap of nickels and dimes. "Just needed starting up, is all," Mr. Anderson said, frowning dubiously at the ornamental cow which is Laurie's bank and at the table knife I had been using to pry my way into it; "Could of done it yourself."

I laughed lightly, as befits a lady who would rather rob a bank than touch a furnace, and said, "And what do I owe you, Mr. Anderson?"

"Dollar'll do it," he said, and watched wide-eyed while

I carefully counted out a dollar in nickels and dimes and swept it off the table and poured it into his hand. "*There* you are," I said. "I hope you don't mind change."

"Well, thanks," Mr. Anderson said. He closed his big hand around the money and carried it that way to the back door, and I followed him, talking with animation about how glad I was that there had been nothing really *wrong* with the furnace, and didn't it look like it might stop raining, after all. Mr. Anderson got into his truck, jingling, and drove off down the driveway without looking back, and I went back to my heap of money and began to set it out in piles of nickels and dimes, humming to myself. I could hardly leave the bank entirely empty, in case Laurie picked it up and expected it to rattle, so I reluctantly returned half a dozen nickels to it. That, it turned out, left me enough to pay the laundryman, but for the garbage man, whom I had completely forgotten, I had to resort to Jannie, who was quite poor, and, with Sally's meagre collection of pennies, left me with forty-three cents in pennies and my original three quarters. Carol came with my loaf of bread and my can of tunafish and resolutely declined to take the pennies, because if she took them home she would only have to put them in *her* penny bank. I had to let the taxi go without paying Mr. Williams, since by that time I had put all the banks carefully back in place and I felt that it might look suspicious to Laurie if I tried paying the taxi fare in pennies. While I was making the creamed tunafish for supper Cliff came to fix the furnace, and I told him that Mr. Anderson had already come, but would he mind getting the top off this jar of mayonnaise? He hit it with a table knife and held it under hot water and tried it in the door jamb and I said I would make a vinegar dressing instead and he said oh, yes, Nancy thought I might like to come over for some bridge tonight; they could get a fourth.

I was about to accept with pleasure when I recalled that our baby-sitter's toll has gone up to forty cents an hour, and since I *had* to have milk money I could afford to play only forty-eight cents worth of bridge, or barely one rubber. So I said, smiling bravely, that I thought I had better stay at home with my fatherless children. Eddie brought my car back about seven; "Carburetor," he said briefly, wiping the steering wheel with a greasy sleeve before getting out. "All set now."

My husband called that night and asked how was everything going, and I said well, the car had broken down and the furnace had gone out and I had run out of money and no one could get the top off the mayonnaise. He asked had he better come right home? and I said of course not, everything was fine *now*, except for the mayonnaise. He was just back from having dinner with friends, he said, and was on his way to a poker game.

I went to bed about ten and lay awake for two hours listening to a funny noise going on somewhere in the cellar or the attic or maybe it was only someone prowling around outside. When I woke up the next morning the sun was out and the children were laughing in the kitchen and I lay in bed for a minute thinking of how a day full of troubles and annoyances, like yesterday, always brought a fine day like today, and I must be sure to remember this in future. Cheerfully I made cream of wheat for breakfast, filled the lunchboxes, brushed the hair, tied the shoes, gathered the books, and got everyone shepherded into the car by twenty after eight. "Well, well," I said, "we're in plenty of time *this* morning."

"Laurie sits with the girls, Laurie sits with the girrrrrrls."

"Now you *listen*–"

"Old Mother *Hubbid*–"

"Children," I said, a smile in my voice, "let's not be cross with one another on such a beautiful day. Let's all be *happy*, and *glad* the *sun* is out. Let's everyone *smile*."

I pressed the starter.

"Cubbid."

I pressed the starter again.

THE INDEFINABLE SENSE of harvest entered the house, of apples to be stored away, of Christmas in the perceptible future. A fever of activity seized me, and I painted the girls' bookcase yellow. The lawn furniture came indoors and I began wondering if the snowsuits could go another winter. One day I brought Jannie home a little silk scarf, blue and pink check, and she accepted it with pleasure, remarking that she would surely, surely wear it to school the next day. She wore it tied fashionably around her neck, in a trim bow, and I pointed it out to her father, who said it looked very nice indeed. The next day she had threaded her little scarf casually through the top buttonhole of her jacket; the day after that she tied it loosely around her hair in back. Wondering, I went off and got myself a little purple scarf. I spent fifteen minutes trying to tie it loosely around my hair in back and it made me look like a chorus girl dressed as a rabbit. I gave my purple scarf to Jannie, and she tied it to her pink and blue one, and wore the two together as a belt around the top of her skirt, from which she had removed the shoulder-straps. The next day she had one tied around her wrist and the other neatly folded on her dresser. Timidly I offered her two more, one gold and one green, and the next day Sally came to breakfast with her hair tied into a topknot with the green one; Jannie was wearing the gold one in *her* hair. I pointed this out to her father, and he said it looked very nice indeed. Emboldened, I came to Jannie with a little white scarf I had bought and asked her to tie up my hair for me and she brought a chair and a hairbrush and worked over me for quite a while, fussing and murmuring and clucking her tongue. Finally she got down and came around and looked at me from the front and sighed and said "Well, go show Daddy." I went and showed Daddy and he looked at me for a long minute and then looked at Jannie, and Jannie shrugged and my husband said to me,

"Whatever happened to that nice blue dress you used to wear? The one I liked?"

I gave the little white scarf to Jannie and went off sullenly and spent the rest of the day mothproofing bathing suits.

Laurie came home from school at about that time with a frightful little ditty which began "Salami was a dancer who danced before the king, and every time she danced she didn't wear a thing . . ." Jannie learned it immediately and they chanted it in chorus. Sally laboriously learned to sing "Jingle Bells."

Two days before his eighth birthday, Laurie rode his bike around a bend, directly into the path of a car. I can remember with extraordinary clarity that one of the people in the crowd which gathered handed me a lighted cigarette, I can remember saying reasonably that we all ought not to be standing in the middle of the road like this, I can remember the high step up into the ambulance. When they told us at the hospital, late that night, that everything was going to be all right, we came home and I finished drying the breakfast dishes. Laurie woke up in the hospital the next morning, with no memory of anything that had happened since breakfast two days before, and he was so upset by the thought that he had ridden in an ambulance and not known about it that the ambulance had to be engaged again to bring him home two weeks later, with the sirens screaming and an extremely proud

Jannie sitting beside him and traffic separating on either side.

We put him, of course, into our bedroom; my mother always used to put sick children into the "big" bed, and I have still that half-remembered feeling that it is one of the signs of being *really* sick, sick enough to stay home from school. My mother, however, never had to cope with anything more complex than my brother's broken arm: I had under my wavering care this active patient with concussion, a broken hand, and various patched-up cuts and bruises; who was not, under doctor's orders, to excite himself, to move his arm; who was not, most particularly, to raise his head or try to turn over; and who was not, it was clearly evident, going to pay any attention to anything the doctor said.

"Now I'm home I can have whatever I want," Laurie announced immediately I arrived in the room with the tray of orange juice, plain toast, and chicken soup which my mother before me believed was the proper basic treatment for an invalid; he cast a disapproving eye at the tray, and said, "Doc said I could have *real* food."

"The most important thing," I told him, "is for you to keep yourself quiet, and warm, and not excited. That dog, for instance."

Toby buried his huge head under the pillow and tried to pretend that he was invisible. "What dog?" said Laurie.

"And," I went on with great firmness, patting Toby absently on the shoulder, "you are absolutely not to lift your head and you are absolutely not to move without help and if you do—"

"I got to go back to the hospital," Laurie said. He wiggled comfortably into the hollow under Toby's chin. "It wasn't so bad there," he said. "*Food* was good, anyway."

"Jannie and Sally are not allowed in this room. No visitors at all for at least a week."

Shax moved softly into the doorway, looked at me and then speculatively at Laurie, and then walked sedately across the room and went up onto the bed, where he settled down without haste next to Laurie's feet, purring. Laurie grinned at me. "Jannie's already *been* here," he said. "She was telling me one of her stories while you were downstairs fixing that junk on the tray, and Sally brought me her teddy bear."

I sighed.

"It's under the covers somewhere," Laurie said. "Doc said you would tell me all about it, all about what happened."

"We won't think about it."

"Doc said I was hit by a car."

"So you were."

"I don't remember." Laurie was accusing. "Seems as though I'd remember *some*thing about it."

"I think it's just as well," I said. "Better to remember pleasant things than sad ones."

"What's so sad about *this?*"

"Keep your head down." I settled back in the armchair and took up my book. "You go to sleep; I'll sit right here."

Laurie closed his eyes obediently, but Toby wriggled and Laurie laughed. "Listen," he said, "tell me about it."

"There's nothing you don't already know," I said. "It's all over, after all."

"Was there a lot of blood?"

"Laurie, surely–"

"*Was* there?"

"There was some," I said reluctantly.

"On the road?"

"Yes. Keep your head down."

"Gee," Laurie said luxuriously. "And the cops–did the cops come? Doc said the cops called him."

"Officer Harrison was there, and he took charge of everything. It was Sunday and he was home cutting his lawn and he came right over when he heard–when it happened."

"When he heard the crash," Laurie said. "Gee, what a noise it must of made."

"Keep your *head* down."

"How many cops?"

"Officer Harrison, and Mr. Lanza, and two or three others I didn't know. I called the State police station and thanked them a few days ago. They were very happy to hear that you were so much better."

"Doc said you fainted."

"I did *not*." I sat up indignantly.

"Did Daddy faint?"

"Certainly not."

"Did Jannie faint?"

"I sent Jannie and Sally down to the Olsons'," I said. "They don't know very much about it."

"I won't tell them," Laurie said reassuringly. "What about my bike–is it all right?"

"Well," I said, "no, it isn't. As a matter of fact, it's broken."

"I *bet* it is," said Laurie, with relish. "Boy, did that bike ever get smacked–I bet it's in a million pieces."

"Keep your head down."

"Hey, what about my clothes?" Laurie said, remembering. "I woke up in the hospital and I had on a nightgown; what about my clothes?"

"Since you're feeling so well," I said, remembering, "I might as well point out that even though I was quite worried about you, I was positively ashamed when they undressed you at the hospital. I distinctly remember telling you to put on clean clothes that morning, and whatever may be said for your shirt, your underwear–"

"They undressed me at the hospital? Who?"

"The nurse. And when I saw that underwear–"

"The *nurse? She* undressed me?"

"Keep your head *down*."

"Oh, brother," said Laurie. He thought, while Toby, his head on the pillow, breathed heavily and happily, and

Shax stirred, lifted his head, and curled up more comfortably. "Where are my clothes now?" Laurie asked finally.

"Your shoes are put neatly—*neatly*—under the chair in your room. That underwear has been sent to the laundry, and your socks and blue jeans, too." I hesitated. "Your shirt was thrown out," I said.

"Why?" Laurie demanded. "*Why* was my shirt thrown out?"

"It was torn," I said.

"Torn? You mean it was covered with blood or something?"

"No," I said. "It was torn. Cut."

"Cut?"

"Keep your head down. They cut it off you at the hospital."

"They did?" Laurie said, his eyes shining. "They had to *cut* it off?"

"Well, they *preferred* to."

"Where is it?"

"I told you, it was thrown out. They gave me your clothes at the hospital and told me the shirt was thrown out."

Laurie asked accusingly, "You didn't keep that shirt? All covered with blood and you didn't *keep* it?"

"Why should I keep it?"

"Which one was it? The green checked one?"

"That was the one you took off in the morning. You put on the new shirt with the baseball picture."

"*That* one? My new one?"

"There are plenty of others," I said, making a mental note about never going near those baseball shirts again. "How about you go to sleep now?"

"That good baseball shirt? And you went and threw it out?"

"You couldn't have worn it again."

"Who wants to *wear* it?" said Laurie. "What else happened?"

"Well," I said, "Brooklyn lost the pennant that same afternoon."

"I heard the Series in the hospital," Laurie said. "What a robbery."

"Would you like to go to sleep now?"

"I bet Dad was nearly crazy," Laurie said.

"Not at all," I said, "he was–"

"Losing the last day like that. Gee," Laurie said, squeezing down between Toby and Shax, "it's not bad being home."

A month later, with satisfaction only secondary to Laurie's, I took him back to school to pick up his books so he could try to catch up on his work. "Remember," I told him in the car before we went into the school, "thank the teacher and the kids for the nice basket they sent you."

"Yeah," Laurie said. He had chosen ten in the morning as the ideal moment to present himself at school.

"And don't forget to thank the teacher for her flowers."

"Yeah."

"And tell her I'll help you at home with arithmetic."

"Come *on*," Laurie said.

We entered the classroom in triumph; Laurie threw open the door and stood for a moment in the doorway before advancing with a swagger Cyrano might have envied. "I'm back," he said into the quiet of the spelling lesson.

"Thank you *so* much for the flowers," I told the teacher. "Laurie appreciated them *so* much."

Laurie sat on one of the front desks, holding his hand with the traction splint prominently displayed. All the third-grade girls gathered around him, and the boys sat on the floor and on nearby desks. "–And I guess there were five hundred people there," he was saying, "they came tearing in from all over. And the street–you oughta seen the street–*covered* with blood–"

"I'll go over his arithmetic with him," I told the teacher.

"He was doing splendidly," she said absently, her eyes on Laurie.

"–And my good shirt, they had to *cut* it off me, ten doctors, and there was so much blood on it they had to throw it away because it was all cut to pieces and bloody. And I went in an ambulance with the sireens and boy! did *we* travel. Boy!"

"And will he need to go over his reading?"

"Excuse me," said Laurie's teacher. Unwillingly, she moved closer to the spellbinder, her hand still reassuringly on my arm. "And my mother fainted," he was saying, "and my *father* . . ."

THREE

Sometimes, in my capacity as mother, I find myself sitting open-mouthed and terrified before my own children, little individual creatures moving solidly along in their own paths and yet in some mysterious manner vividly reminiscent of a past which my husband and I know we have never communicated to them; I remember the little shock of familiarity I felt when I first saw Jannie skip down the front walk, and the sense of lost years slipping past, unrealized, when Laurie came home chanting "O U T spells out, and out you go, down to the bottom of the deep blue sea with a dirty dishrag turned inside *out*," although there was a heated family discussion about the second line of "Ibbitty, Bibbitty, Sibbitty, Sab," because Laurie believed that it went "Ibbitty, bibbitty, conoso," and *I* said it was "conothco," and my husband said it was "Ibbitty, bibbitty, canarsie," and it reminded me of the little idiocy which went "Laurie bumbaurie tiliaurie gosaurie," although my husband said that *that* one ended "gotaurie." Sally discovered in herself the ability to chant that most basic and most jeering of childhood tunes, the "*da*, da, da-*da*, da," or "*I* know a *se*cret," melody; Laurie began collecting pictures of baseball players, which came enclosed in packages of bubble gum; in my day they used to be in packages of licorice. The candy cigarette turned up, and the chocolate apple; they no longer give away baseball bats with pairs of new shoes, but Buster Brown still grins with his dog from the soles. A whole section of forgotten past came back, for instance, one evening when Laurie remarked joyfully that a house near the school had a ghost in it and none of the kids from school would walk past it, although one intrepid adventurer named Oliver maintained that he had been inside and had of course seen the ghost, and "Boy," Laurie said with reminiscent pleasure, "was *he* scared!"

My husband and I looked at one another; in my case it was a house on the next block—the one next to the vacant lot—and the boy who said he had been inside was named Andy Young (how is it that I have not forgotten Andy Young in all these years?) and my husband remembered that there was a shack at the back of the school yard which had a ghost in it and that one Louie Fair had been inside. In all cases the punchline of the story was precisely, "Boy, was *he* scared!" My husband and I found ourselves repeating the same amused platitudes about boys who went into haunted houses that our parents had used to us, Laurie retorted that *every*one knew this house was haunted and he bet *we* wouldn't go inside, and there was a familiar split-second hesitation before my husband and I answered, in chorus, that *certainly* we would go inside, if it were not that the house belonged to someone else who would presumably resent our entering without permission. Laurie said Boy, he bet a ghost was sure a scarey thing to see, and his father offered to compose a document demonstrating that our house was haunted if Laurie would take copies of this document and distribute them, like handbills, around the neighborhood. Laurie agreed with delight, and the conversation closed, in traditional style, with the flat statement that Laurie was not to go into the haunted house under any circumstances since it was a) someone else's property and b) if abandoned, probably dangerous, with broken glass and falling beams. Point c) was not mentioned, but I personally have always believed in ghosts; I taught Laurie later a small charm against evil spirits, disguising it as a nursery rhyme. The handbill * was duly composed and Laurie set out with it, although along the way he fell in with evil spirits against whom his charm was powerless and played two innings of softball; when his father asked him later about the handbill he said that Mrs. Wright, down the road, had read it and thought it was very clever and asked Laurie if he had written it himself. Mrs. Collins had not had time to read it right then but said she would send

* See Appendix.

over a plate of cookies later. By the time school started again in the fall, gang warfare had taken over the fourth grade and the ghost was allowed to languish in his haunted house, untroubled again by Oliver, although I daresay that when someday Laurie's son remarks that a friend of *his* has explored a haunted house, Oliver's name will come, freely and with nostalgia, to Laurie's mind.

The opening of school that fall found Sally, scorning the overalls which now read ~~LAURIE JANNIE~~ SALLY, preparing to enter upon nursery school. Jannie's girls had all retired abruptly to a ranch in Texas, from which they very rarely wrote illegible letters to their mother, but Sally now had a house of her own, located approximately and damply in the middle of the river near *our* house; we all heard a great deal about this retreat of Sally's, in which a number of small children Sally's age lived in utter happiness upon lollipops and corn on the cob. Sally visited there, she explained, at night after the rest of us were asleep, and when she was particularly angry with any of us she shouted furiously, "*You* can't come to *my* house!"

Sally had at this time entered with complete abandon into a form-fitting fairyland; I saw her sometimes as wandering perpetually in a misty odd world, where familiar shapes merged and changed as she passed and occasionally a brother or a sister or a parent, stepping from behind a tree, might briefly interrupt her journey; with the exception of Jannie, who slept in the same room and had no refuge from Sally's bedroom stories, I spent more time with Sally than with anyone else, and began to find that a large part of my daily activity was accompanied by Sally's tuneful and unceasing conversation; part song, part story, part uncomplimentary editorial comment. Around the house, my head deep in a pillowcase or the oven, my eyes focussed on that supernatural neatness which the housewife sees somehow shadowing her familiar furniture, it was largely possible to disregard, or not-quite-hear, Sally, but in the car I was entirely what I believe is called a captive audience. We traveled far afield that fall, Sally and I, up and down familiar and unfamiliar roads, going perhaps after pumpkins, or taking a side road because for a minute it looked unusually yellow to Sally, or just going the longest way around because it took us over a covered bridge crossing Sally's river and people living nearby owned a baby goat. "In my river," Sally remarked once, chillingly, "we sleep in wet beds, and we hear our mothers calling us,"–giving me a sudden terrifying picture of my own face, leaning over the water, wavering, and my voice far away and echoing; "The water is probably *extremely* cold," I told her, and shivered. "In the river," Sally said, "no one ever comes except *us*." We drove upon occasion, Sally and I, up and down Murphy's Hill, which was every bit as steep going up as it was going down and led only to a kind of plateau neatly edged with trees; in the fall these trees presented an appearance sufficiently startling to make a trip up (and of course down) Murphy's Hill a rewarding experience even beyond its roller coaster aspects; the vines on the trunks of these trees turned red early, and the trees stayed green late, and a row of straight, youthful green trees with bright red trunks was a sight I have never seen *except* at the top of Murphy's Hill.

Sally habitually rode standing on her head in the back seat, and gave every sign of regarding me as perhaps an additional fixture to the car, a sort of extension of the steering wheel; her conversation included me casually, and my comments became a sort of counterpoint to which she attended when it was necessary, perhaps, to find a rhyme, or perfect a rhythm; we found ourselves one day on a back road, turning a corner suddenly into a herd of cows.

"Do you know who I am?" Sally was singing, on her head in the back seat, "DO YOU KNOW WHO I AM?"

The cows were wandering vaguely—very much, I suppose, in the manner of cows unsupervised and not in the least pleased about it; they crowded the road and moved in all directions at once. "I'm a rat and you're a fish," Sally sang, "and now you know who I am."

"Do turn yourself rightside up," I said. "The road is covered with cows and I can't see out the back window."

There was nothing to do, of course, but stop the car and wait until some avenue opened itself through the cows. I am earnestly afraid of all large animals; I closed the car windows tight and cringed in my seat, entirely convinced that a cow was going to try to climb onto, or into, the car. "Look at all the cows," I said to Sally with a sort of wild gaiety; I did not, after all, want to communicate to a small child my fears, which might possibly be unfounded; "I guess you never saw *this* many cows before."

"*These* are not cows," Sally said. "*These* are giants."

"See how they stop and look at us," I remarked airily, moving over into the center of the front seat. "I suppose *they* wonder what *we* are." I grinned back convulsively at a bovine face next to the window. "Nice cow," I said.

"Lots and lots and *lots* of giants, and when *I* see giants I know their mothers are coming to eat me."

This corresponded so nearly to my own apprehensions that, wildly disregarding the probable suicidal result of frightening a herd of cows into a stampede, I slammed my hand down onto the horn and my foot onto the gas pedal. The cows backed away and turned, lumbering against one another, and finally determined unanimously on one direction, which was down the road ahead of us; running, so that with Sally calling encouragement from a rear window and me leaning on the horn, we found ourselves in the odd position of chasing a herd of cows swiftly down a country road. "Run, giants, run," Sally shouted out the window. I made a broad screaming turn onto a side road and pulled up, panting and listening to the thunder of hooves as the cows made off into the distance. "Golly," I said.

"Giants are very nice sometimes," Sally remarked, turning herself upside down, "and sometimes giants are not very nice and sometimes giants are very nice and sometimes giants are–"

It was the day of Sally's fingers, I think, when we went to get the apples. There was a farm not far away where they sold an honest frost-bitten apple and had a speckled hen in a cage, and Sally and I made it, that fall, one of our regular stopping-off places; Sally was always given an apple to eat, and I always admired the speckled hen, and we came home with the car full of apples and their rich scent; on this day Sally had amused herself by counting the fingers on her left hand, which came out six, and the fingers in her glove, which came out five, and she was deeply involved in the problem of accommodating her fingers into the glove, which had unreasonably fit perfectly until now; the road was narrow and winding, and I was humming to myself and watching the way the sun came through the colored trees. We moved without any recognition of danger onto a scene of fire; I realized as we came around a corner that there had been a vague sense of activity and noise ahead, but as I slowed down the wild approach of the fire engine sounded behind me and I had no choice but to pull my car quickly over into the ditch as the engine rushed by. So there we sat, Sally and I, in the car, unable to turn and go back the way we had come, surely unable to go forward, and–I, at least–most unwilling to stay where we were. "Is it a giant?" Sally asked uncertainly, coming over into the front seat to look out, "is it a giant, or what?"

"It's a fire," I said. "That farmhouse is burning."

"Why?" Sally asked.

I thought fleetingly that perhaps this would be a good time to warn Sally against playing with matches, but my moment had passed; "It looks like a giant to *me*," she said. "Are we going to stay here?"

"Until the road ahead is clear," I said. "We've got to wait till those other cars get out of the way, because we can't turn around."

"Then I will have another apple," Sally said. She returned to the back seat, found an apple, and stood herself up on her head. "I am going to sing an apple song," she said.

We had to stay there for over an hour; it was quite a fire. Had the farmer whose home was burning been of a philosophical turn—which I am fairly sure he was not—and believed that he was due for at least one fire during his lifetime and was having it now, he might have taken great consolation in the way this one came off; his livestock, I learned from brief bulletins from the firemen, was safe, his children securely at school, his wife and farmhands unharmed, his insurance invulnerable, and as we arrived they had been carrying out his television set. The sound country policy of letting the burning house go and trying to save the buildings nearby was being put into practice; the fire hose stretched nicely to Sally's river, and although the house and barn, which were close to one another and both hopelessly lost, flamed ominously, the firemen were successfully soaking down the other outbuildings and the one or two neighboring houses. There was not even a wind.

"I'm a sweetie," Sally sang, "I'm a honey, I'm a poppacorn, I'm a potato chip, all my days for you."

My principal feeling, beyond the primitive terror of the fire itself, was of embarrassment. I was deeply concerned lest these people assume that we, my daughter and I, had come curiously to watch their fire. I wanted very much to catch hold of one of the firemen and explain that we were here entirely by accident, like the fire itself; we had been passing by, I would tell him, on our way home from buying apples, and had been caught by chance on this road; we did not ordinarily race fire engines to fires, I would go on, but in this case, what with the narrow road . . .

"Aren't they through *yet?*" Sally demanded over my shoulder.

"Almost," I said. "The fire engine is getting ready to leave."

"We shouldn't of stayed *this* long," Sally said.

I pulled out of the ditch, and waved cheerily to the farmer's wife as we went by. We reached home to find the rest of our family waiting restlessly for dinner.

"We got apples," I said to my husband, "and we saw—"

"*Giants.*" Sally swung wildly on her father's arm, "*Giants.*" She nodded.

"Giants?" my husband asked me, staring.

"There was a big giant party and they were cooking marshmallows," Sally said. She caught Jannie in a long ominous look. "*Giant* marshmallows." Her voice dropped to a compelling whisper. "And the giants were all stamping around and the *mother* giant sat there and watched them, and the mother giant said 'Wait till those other cars get out of the way and then we can go home.' And I had ninety-seven apples. And we came over the river and the mother giant went in and got drowned dead." There was a short, respectful silence.

Finally Laurie inquired of his father, "Who was Aristides the Just?"

"Friend of your mother's," my husband said absently. "Apple pie?" he said hopefully to me.

"I got to do a report," Laurie said.

"Y'know something?" Jannie asked me. She glanced around at her younger sister and then went on in a low voice, "I don't believe it when Sally tells about giants. Do you?"

"Certainly not," I said. "She's just making it up." And recognized clearly that there was no ring of conviction whatever in my voice. "My goodness," I said heartily, "who's afraid of *giants?*"

During that fall the conflict of individual cultures in our family became explicit, and uncontrollable. My husband and I, a little frayed after a number of years spent—it seems—almost entirely in the society of small children, had managed to build up little sets of foibles which we were reluctant to sacrifice. Laurie had developed opinions which could only be called decided. Sally had not so far seen any reason for doubting that anything could be achieved if you just made enough noise about it. Jannie, who had never in her life doubted anything she said herself although no parental pronouncements sounded to her entirely impartial or, no matter how emphatic, reasonable, entered first grade that fall and came into contact with the public school system.

Now, I have nothing against the public school system as it is presently organized, once you allow the humor of its basic assumption about how it is possible to teach things to children, and my experiences with Laurie have convinced me that the schools are well enough, and my children are well enough, and it is only any chance combination of these two which is apt to become explosive. Laurie succeeded in fighting his way to the fourth grade without showing any noticeable signs of contact with education, but Jannie brought up against the school an impact which must have been felt in the very bedrock of learning, and which certainly put a crack in the family hearthstone.

I had been warned that when a little girl goes to school she prefers to wear dresses and pigtails, but Jannie thought she would rather wear shorts the first day, and an old baseball hat of Laurie's. I struggled out of bed on the morning which was to see Jannie off to school for the first time and combed my hair and dressed myself with the idea of appearing before teachers and other mothers, escorting my daughter, but Jannie told me at breakfast, "If I am going to go to school at *all,* I think I would prefer to go by myself."

After five busy years I no longer attempted to argue with Jannie before breakfast; I nodded and slipped my shoes off under the breakfast table. "You don't mind my coming to the door to wave goodbye to you, I suppose?" I asked, and Jannie, considering, said, "If you don't cry or something."

"Do I have to take *her* to school?" Laurie demanded. "On the bus and all?"

Laurie regarded the new school bus as his personal and exclusive conveyance. "She's got to go to school," I said. "They don't let children grow up and not go to school."

Laurie, regarding his sister, laughed bitterly, and Jannie said, "I believe I'll sit in the other end of the bus from Laurie. I don't care for unpolite boys."

"Do I have to hold her hand?" Laurie asked.

"Certainly you do not," Jannie said. "I prefer to go by myself, thank you. If I am going to school at *all,* that is."

The notion that she might, upon consideration, decide not to go to school at all, was enough for me. "Will you be careful?" I asked.

"Once," Jannie remarked exclusively to Sally, "I had a friend named Susan, and Susan went to the horse racing and she betted on a horse named Susan, and the horse fell through the side of the track and all the horses went to see if he was all right and he had broken the gate and all the men got away and the horses couldn't catch them to bring them back."

"Ah," said Sally intelligently. "*You* can't come to *my* house."

I had no trouble not crying when Jannie left; after all these years during which I have seen one child or another go off to one place or another and managed to control myself except during major crises like Cub Scout award meetings and nursery school Dancing Days—after all these years my goodbye kiss and my wave from the front window no longer exhibit more than the mildest apprehension. Jannie climbed stoutly into the school bus, her brother behind her pretending unsuccessfully that she was just some girl who happened to get on at the same stop he did, and I saw Jannie's head move down the bus to a seat at the end. "Sister's gone to school," I said to Sally.

"Ah," said Sally. "And will she come home again?"

Laurie reported, when he came home at three o'clock, that although he looked for her, and waited at the bus, and even, with some faint vestige of fraternal feeling, asked a couple kids if they had seen his sister, Jannie had not got on the bus, and at four o'clock I was driving back and forth between our house and the school for the sixth time when I saw Jannie wandering and singing along the side of the road. I stopped the car next to her and leaped out, babbling, and she took my hand amiably and said, "I think school will be all right for me, after all."

"Where have you *been?*" I said.

"I followed my teacher home," Jannie said. "I wanted to see where she lived."

At the end of her second week in first grade Jannie remarked one evening at the dinner table, "Mrs. Skinner says paper napkins are vulgar." Mrs. Skinner is the first grade teacher, and it had already, by then, begun to get through to the rest of us that Mrs. Skinner's opinions, relayed through Jannie, were inclined to be vehement, positive, and perhaps even a shade on the critical side. "Mrs. Skinner," Jannie went on, eyeing her brother, "says little boys are made of snails."

"Who's little?" Laurie demanded, stung. "Seems to me–"

"I *beg* your humble pardon," said Jannie–"I beg your humble pardon" is another Skinnerism–"I beg your *humble* pardon, but Mrs. Skinner says that boys any size are made of snails and little girls like Sally and me–"

"Sally and I," said Laurie.

"I *beg* your humble pardon. –like Sally and me are dainty and sweet."

"Huh," said Laurie eloquently.

"And now I think of it, what's so vulgar about paper napkins?" I wanted to know.

"Mrs. Skinner," Jannie said gently, "doesn't care if you *use* paper napkins. Mrs. Skinner will let you use paper napkins if you *want* to. But then you're just *vulgar*, is all."

"Some people," Laurie remarked, addressing his plate,

"Some people just think they know everything, I really do believe. Some people just think they know *every*thing."

"Jannie and me are dainty and sweet, *are*n't we, Jannie?" Sally gestured with her fork, scattering green peas generously onto the table. "And Laurie is full of snails."

"Children, be quiet," my husband said firmly. "Mother and I want to talk." He addressed me through a profound silence. "Did you sew the button on my shirt?" he enquired.

"Water with the meal," Jannie murmured, "is unsanitary."

We had been exposed to Mrs. Skinner from about the third day of school, when Jannie came home with a mimeographed sheet of paper containing her instructions for conduct in the first grade; she was not, I noted from the paper, to come to school with dirty fingernails, broken shoelaces, or odorous lunches. She was to wear dresses or skirts. ("Mrs. Skinner says girls wearing pants are vulgar.") Her hair was to be cut short or braided, her socks matching, and no pins were to be in evidence. ("How about a dental plate for that missing front tooth?" I asked impolitely, and Jannie smiled at me with sweet tolerance.) She was not to wear jewelry (vulgar) or earmuffs. If she intended to visit anyone after school, or to sniffle moderately (immoderate or obtrusive sniffling was not countenanced) or to require a container of milk with her lunch, she was to bring a note. If her shoes needed soling, or she squinted at the blackboard, or created a disturbance during Songtime, Mrs. Skinner would send a note back. No parent was, under any circumstances whatsoever, for any reason up to and including absolute national emergency, to visit the classroom at any time except—Mrs. Skinner's unwilling bow to the school authorities and their tyranny—during Parent's Visiting Week. Children were not encouraged to discuss their home life at school.

"Mrs. Skinner says," Jannie remarked as her father read the mimeographed notice for the third apoplectic time, "that men who smoke are vulgar, especially cigars."

It did not take us very long to find out that Mrs. Skinner thought that raised voices, dining in restaurants, and playing cards were all vulgar. Jannie took to keeping care of her own socks and she bathed every night, and once a week, while we were out carousing at our regular bridge game, she washed her hair inefficiently. "A girl," she told me, "who does not keep herself clean is unwomanly."

"Talking about being clean is vulgar," I told her nastily.

"Clean talk," said Jannie, "is womanly."

"I beg your *humble* pardon," I said.

"Granted," said Jannie.

"This is unbearable," I said to my husband, after Jannie had set out her clean dress for tomorrow with her clean socks, and had cleaned her fingernails and gone to bed, "this is positively vulgar—I mean unbearable."

"What's so vulgar about keeping your hands in your pockets, is what *I* want to know?" my husband said unhappily, looking up from a book catalogue. "I *have* to put my hands in my pockets *some*times; I keep my cigarettes and my wallet and my handkerchief—"

"Smoking is unsanitary anyway," I said.

"Cats give you colds," Jannie remarked the next afternoon when she came home from school; she dropped her jacket into the center of the hall floor and made an ostentatious large circle around poor old Shax, who raised his head and stared at her with honest surprise. "Cats give you colds and dogs give you mange."

"Now, *look*, young lady," I said sternly, "you go right out and pick up your jacket and apologize to Shax. You haven't had a cold since—"

"I *beg* your humble pardon. Mrs. Skinner says cats give you colds."

"Cats do *not*—"

"It's vulgar to contradict."

During a fairly stormy dinner, during which Laurie fled the table in a blind fury, shouting, "What the *hell* do I have to be womanly *for?*" Jannie succeeded in eliminating string beans (unsanitary), coffee (unhealthy), and the clearing of the table by the lady of the house (vulgar). She told her father while I was bringing in the dessert and setting a tray to take upstairs to Laurie that we must really get a housekeeper.

"Who is going to pay for this housekeeper?" her father asked, the way he always asks me.

"Speaking of money is vulgar," Jannie said.

Sally, who demonstrated the far-reaching arm of Mrs.

Skinner by preserving an awed silence when her sister spoke, and by even making some abortive attempts to keep herself clean, said now, "*I*'m dainty, aren't I? Can I have more dessert?"

" 'May,' dear," Jannie said. "*We* say '*May* I have more dessert.' " She implied pointedly by her tone that her father and mother habitually and vulgarly used 'can,' as we do. "Dear Mother," she went on—"Dear Mother" is, I hardly need point out, Mrs. Skinner's presumable manner of addressing *her* mother—"I need two buttons sewed on my jacket before tomorrow. Mrs. Skinner says that if you thread the needle for me I can do them as well as *you* do."

"You may tell Mrs. Skinner," I said tensely, "that I have quite enough to do with the dinner dishes and drawing your—" I hesitated, deleting a vulgar word "—bath, without sitting down to teach you to sew. You may tell Mrs. Skinner that if she is so—" I deleted again "—womanly *she* can teach you to sew. And furthermore—"

"A lady who does not know how to sew nicely is—"

My husband and I flipped a coin—secretly, because money is vulgar and gambling is unwomanly and our expressed opinions were, to say the least, unsanitary—to decide which of us would stop by during Parent's Visiting Week and beard Mrs. Skinner. My husband lost, but I had to promise to stand right outside the door while he was talking to Mrs. Skinner and rush in if he were cornered.

The morning his father was to attend school Jannie looked

him over carefully. "I told you a million times that standing with your hands in your pockets is *vulgar*," she said. "And even though you're made of snails you don't have to—"

"Show it," my husband said miserably. "I suppose it's this tie."

"The tie's all *right*," Jannie said without conviction, and sighed. "I wish you'd sort of give up Parent's Day this month," she said. "I'm going to have a real spell of faintness waiting for you in the car."

I stood outside the door of the first grade room, with a clear view of the health chart on the front blackboard and the row of trim geraniums on the window sill, and I heard Mrs. Skinner saying clearly, in a voice which carried beautifully across the empty desks and out into the hall, but in a voice also not raised and not in the least, I am sorry to say, vulgar, "Your little Joanne is a charming child, charming. So refined." She lowered her voice slightly. "*You* know, sir, that there are children in every class, and from every walk of life, mind you, who are coarse. Who are even unclean."

"Vulgar, I suppose," my husband said.

"Precisely." I could almost hear Mrs. Skinner glowing with satisfaction. "Vulgar, precisely the word I was hesitating to use. But little Joanne . . ." her voice died off tenderly.

"How about your own children?" my husband asked.

"They are many of them unbelievably charming, of

course," Mrs. Skinner said, "but of course from every walk of life . . ."

"No," my husband said, "your *own* children. Children you've—well—*had* yourself."

"I regret to say," Mrs. Skinner said with a soft wistfulness, "that we have not been blessed—"

"Not having children is unwomanly," my husband said, "in a woman."

"True, true," Mrs. Skinner said, and sighed again. "My spells of faintness," she said; "my unfortunate weak limbs . . . but," she added brightly, "you did not want to hear about *my* troubles, sir. We were speaking of your little Joanne—such a charming child."

"However," my husband said relentlessly, "I presume that had you been blessed with little charmers of your own they would have caught colds from cats?"

"I beg your pardon?"

"I beg your *humble* pardon," my husband said. "Is Jannie doing all right in her school work?"

"She is excellent in cleanliness—I don't believe I ever saw a child so conscientious about her nails; her imaginative qualities are unusually good, and so is her general gracefulness. Her singing voice, however . . ."

"How about spelling? Arithmetic?"

"I beg your *humble* pardon?"

"Granted," said my husband.

I tiptoed away at this point, and joined Jannie in the car. While she fidgeted nervously I smoked a cigarette with abandon, dropping ashes on the car seat. After about half an hour my husband came out of the school building; he had his hands in his pockets and he was whistling. "Well?" I asked him as he got into the car, "what happened?"

"Were you all *right?*" Jannie said urgently, "did you *do* anything?"

He untied his tie and draped it over the mirror, took a cigar out of his pocket and put it rakishly into the side of his mouth, and then he turned and grinned at us.

"Curiosity," he said, "is unwomanly."

The dinner table is, in our house, always the family village green, with the big salt and pepper shakers and the plastic table mats silent if appalled witnesses to the intricate weavings of our several dining personalities: Jannie's place is always set left-handed, my husband and I use oversized coffee cups, and Sally requires at least three paper napkins; the dinner, which is cooked by me, tends to be largely upon Sally's level and liberally adorned with chili sauce by Laurie. That night at dinner, Jannie was silent and oppressed. When Laurie pointed out virtuously that she had not touched her dinner, she barely raised her eyes. When Sally observed that Jannie was an impulent girl she did not turn her head, when her father offered her the band from his cigar she gazed sadly upon the ceiling.

"Jannie is invited to Helen's birthday party on Saturday," I informed the table brightly.

"How about I read you ten chapters in your Oz book?" Laurie asked.

"Jannie can be the new mother," Sally said largely, "and Mommy and I will just be the babies and Laurie is the queen and Daddy is a herd of rabbits."

"You may put an ice cube down my back," my husband said earnestly to Jannie.

"Thank you," Jannie said wanly. "I don't feel much like being happy now, thank you."

"Perhaps if I were to lend you my lapel watch?" I suggested.

"I could even read you *twelve* chapters–"

"*You* can come to *my* house."

"*I* think," Laurie observed critically, "if anyone should *ask* me, *I* think she's getting *spots*."

TWO WEEKS LATER, when Jannie was well over the measles and we were only waiting for Laurie and Sally to catch it, I ventured timidly–again at the dinner table–to point out that her nails were dirty.

"What of it?" demanded Jannie, rendered reckless by two lovely weeks of illness. "You think *I* care?"

"What's your name?" Sally asked her.

"Puddentane," Jannie said.

"Where do you live?"

"Down the lane," said Jannie.

"You must keep your nails clean," I said gently, "even if–"

"What's your name?" Sally asked Laurie.

"Laurence," said Laurie.

"Pudden*tane*," Sally said. "When I ask you 'What's your name?' you must say 'Puddentane.' Now what's your name?"

"Laurence."

"Puddentane," Sally shouted, "you bad bad webbis."

"*You* bad bad webbis."

"I am *not* a webbis, *I* said puddentane; I *always* say puddentane. What's *your* name?" she said plaintively to her father.

"Puddentane," he said diplomatically.

"Where do you live?"

"Did you call the health officer?" my husband said to me.

"You bad bad webbis," Sally said reproachfully to Laurie.

"Can I please leave my potato and my meat and my beans?" Jannie asked me. "I don't feel really well *yet*, you know, and I'll eat my bread and butter."

"Eat three mouthfuls of everything," I said. "If they're going to catch it," I told my husband, "there's nothing *we* can do."

"Penicillin?" he said vaguely.

"*That's* no good against measles," Laurie said.

"If I had been addressing you, young man," his father began, "I can assure you that I would have–"

"I couldn't overhelp hearing," Laurie said meekly.

"What's your name?"

"What it comes down to," I said, "is that they might as well have it now as–" I broke off abruptly with a squawk as Sally poked me vigorously with her fork.

"I said 'What's your name?' " Sally reminded me.

"She's too young to have a fork," my husband said. "Little girls should be seen and not heard," he told Sally.

"You bad bad webbis," Sally said gratuitously to her brother.

"If Sally came down with a high fever," my husband said dreamily, "and Laurie came down with a high fever and–"

"Why don't we get a new outside?" Sally asked. "This morning, it was raining and raining." She thought. "And there was a lion on the front porch," she said.

"Really?" said Jannie. "Really, was there a lion on the front porch?"

"Cernly," Sally said.

Laurie put down his fork and turned to his father. "What is long and hard and wears shoes?" he asked. "Bet you a dime you can't guess it."

His father said tentatively, "A horse?"

Laurie guffawed. "Make it twenty cents," he said.

"Surely there was a lion on the front porch," Sally said

to Jannie, "and I saw him and he was walking around very softerly and he ate all the cats and part of the fence."

Jannie addressed me. "*I* was sick in bed, you know," she said. "Was there *really* a lion out there?"

"A horseshoe stake?" my husband said desperately.

"That," Laurie said with relish, "will be twenty cents."

"But a horseshoe stake is long and hard and it wears–" my husband said. "Look, don't the shoes go *around* it?"

"A sidewalk," Laurie said. "It *wears* shoes, see? Now, for another dime, what goes under the water, over the water, and doesn't get wet?"

"I left my rubbers somewhere," my husband said to me.

"You must ask *me* what's my name," Sally said to Laurie.

"What's your name?"

"Tiger," Sally said. "You snick," she told him.

Laurie said triumphantly to his father, who was scowling doggedly at his empty dessert dish, "An old woman crossing a bridge with a pail of water on her head, and counting yesterday and the money you lost to me on the checkers game that's two-seventy-five, and counting my allowance tomorrow that makes two-eighty-five, and the dime you bet me you could eat your bread and butter without using your hands."

"And when you dropped the book and the feather down the stairs," Jannie said.

"Galileo," Laurie told her approvingly, "I forgot. You had a dollar," he said to his father, "that the heavy object and the light object would . . ." he hesitated, looking at me.

"Fall at the same rate of speed," I said helpfully. "It looked like a sure thing."

"Damn it," my husband said, goaded, "I can show you in the book—"

"And twelve cents," Laurie went on inexorably, "for swatting twelve hundred flies."

"*That* wasn't twelve hundred flies," my husband said, "Mother counted them."

"You *gave* them to me to count," I said, "but—"

"*I* can count to twelve hundred," Jannie said. "One, two, three, four, five, six, seven . . ."

"Showing off," I said vengefully, "is vulgar."

"What?" Jannie said.

"Where do you live?"

"Down the lane," said my husband sadly.

"Four ninety-seven," said Laurie, who had been figuring silently.

"Mother will give it to you," my husband said.

DIABOLICALLY, BOTH SALLY and Laurie refused to catch measles after I had gone out and purchased a new thermometer and a large bottle of calamine lotion. My husband and I agreed that it was time that Laurie's natural curiosity about things which did not belong to him should be channelized into a healthy pattern, and that he should be encouraged to give up spending nickels for packs of gum and begin, instead, a coin collection. I did not, at that time—in fact, it seemed like a good idea—perceive any of the parallels which have occurred to me since; the similarity, for instance, between coin collecting and a grasping curiosity about things which do not belong to you, the unfortunate similarity between coins and money; I remember agreeing with my husband that coins were preferable as a collection to, say, stamps, because they wouldn't blow away, or match folders because coins, at least, had some intrinsic value. I remember even saying laughingly that if anything were to be collected, for heaven's sake it might as well be *money*.

My husband and Laurie began on a small scale. I went to the bank and got a roll of nickels and a roll of dimes and a roll of pennies, and they spent an evening examining mint marks and dates and relative condition, and I sat peacefully over my book smiling at them occasionally and thinking how good it was that they should be interested together in such a grown-up fashion. They sent for some little books, named dime books and penny books and nickel books, and each book had a series of little holes large enough for the proper coins, and all coin collectors have to do is find the right coin for the right little hole and put it in. After a while my husband was going to the bank himself with a briefcase. He would get all the money we had changed into coins and then he and Laurie would take all the coins they needed for their books and give me the rest, and I would go out and pay for my groceries in the nickels and dimes which were not needed for the books.

I have never objected to money, as such. But after a while it became necessary to get a huge metal box to keep the coins in, and every mail began to bring heavy little packages of coins from Ruritania and Atlantis and it was suddenly abruptly clear to Jannie and Sally and me that their father and Laurie were planning to get hold of all the money in the world and put it away in their metal box, and a consequent strong bitterness began to show itself around the house. I began to make pointed comments about the last time I had seen a five-dollar bill, and I repeated several times at dinner what the grocer had said to me about people holding up a line at the counter because they had to count out seventeen dollars and thirty-six cents in dimes and nickels and pennies. Jannie took to sleeping with her penny bank under her pillow, and Sally, with a pretty wit, fell to bringing her father small stones and pieces of glass and play money which she embezzled at nursery school. I spent a bag of silver to buy my husband a Piece of Eight for a Christmas present, and had trouble hiding it, since Christmas was still quite a while off, until I thought of keeping it in my pocketbook. Even Sally learned to say "numismatist"; Laurie learned the Greek alphabet from Greek coins and one day turned in his spelling homework done entirely in Greek letters, confounding his schoolmates and thoroughly annoying his teacher.

One Saturday morning an intensely awaited package of coins arrived, and I had to pay thirty-one cents duty charges on it; while I was irritably counting out the money for the postman, Sally took the mail into the study where Laurie and his father were rearranging their classifications, and when I came stamping into the study shouting "Don't we pay enough for this money without—" I found Laurie and his father sitting one on either side of the coffee table, Laurie rocking back and forth and moaning, and his father holding his head in his hands and saying "Oh, no," over and over, and Jannie and Sally regarding them with unwilling sympathy.

"Something wrong?" I asked brightly.

"Something wrong?" Jannie repeated.

"Wrong?" Sally asked.

"Yes," said my husband.

"Look at these darned old *coins*," Laurie said, almost in tears. We looked at the heap of coins on the table, Jannie and Sally and I.

"They're *mixed*," Laurie said.

"Well, my goodness," I told him, "it certainly wouldn't be much fun *collecting* coins if all you did was just put them in the little books and put them in the cabinet. My goodness, half the *fun* in collecting coins—"

My husband raised his head and looked at me. "Listen," he said wanly, "what we ordered was two lots of coins from the same place. One of them was a lot of a hundred and fifty assorted coins of the world."

"Splendid," I said. "I suppose they cost—"

"The other," my husband said, raising his voice, "was a lot of a hundred assorted *counterfeit* coins of the world. And the boxes," he said, "the boxes . . ." He put his head back in his hands.

"They broke," Laurie said. "We got two hundred and fifty coins. Assorted. Mixed."

"Splendid," I said again. "Then all you have to do is sort the counterfeit coins into *one* pile and the *real* coins into *another*—"

"Yeah," Laurie said. "Daddy doesn't feel very well."

This did not seem like the time to enforce my rightful claims to thirty-one cents, so I collected the rest of the mail and left the study with the girls. We sat down on the couch in the living room and opened a letter from the electric company and bills from three department stores and an announcement of the annual fund drive of the Boy Scouts and a pamphlet from a toy company. This last caught the attention of the girls, and we opened it to read. It turned out to be one of those maddening documents in which the desire of children to play with toys is explained and justified, and the desire of parents to buy toys for their children is made painless by a sugar-coating of sound educational advice; "The child's natural impulses are harmlessly directed—" I read, under a picture of a hammering set, and, with a block set, "Little fingers learn busily sense of balance . . ." "Ar," I said, through my teeth.

"What does it say?" Jannie asked. "Read it to us."

The center of the pamphlet was occupied by an article entitled "Healthy Children are Happy Children" or else "Happy Children are Healthy Children," and there was a picture of a sweet-faced mother bending earnestly over her child, guiding his little fingers as they learned a busy sense of balance with a set of blocks. "Who's *that?*" Jannie asked, leaning over to see, "who's that lady? What's she doing?"

I consulted the article. "Children are naturally cooperative and reasonable," I read at random.

"What?"

"*That* means that little girls like you and Sally and boys like Laurie *like* to do things right. That you *want* to learn the best and nicest ways to act."

"I *do?*"

"*I* don't," said Sally emphatically.

"That's not reasonal," Jannie said critically. "Like eating with my fingers; I want to eat with my *fingers*."

"I think the people who wrote this would *let* you eat with your fingers," I said. "Constructive something-or-other."

"Hah," said Jannie.

"Only snicks," Sally opined. "Only snicks."

"Children are happier and better adjusted," I read

grimly, "when given responsibility. The feeling of participating—"

"*I* know," Jannie said. "Pick up your room, set the table, hang up your jacket, brush your teeth, wash—"

"No good," Sally said. "*Not* washing."

"—your hands, put away your toys, fold your napkin—"

"And it means that when I ask you to run upstairs to get me a handkerchief you should go cheerfully," I said, patting her on the head.

"You just read more of that," Jannie said. "I don't think it's sensal at all, except about eating with my fingers."

"Parents should never show anger before the child," I read. "Parents should never show anger before the child. Parents—"

"Hah," Jannie said again.

"Run in the study, dear," I said. "Ask Dad how he's coming with his coins."

"Not *me*," Sally said. "Not *me*."

"But *you*—" Jannic said.

"I do *not*," I said. "I never show anger at all, except that you and your sister and your brother can be far and away the most irritating, the most infuriating, the most maddening—"

"Snicks."

"Snicks," I said. I took a deep breath. "Anyway," I went on, "it says here that Sixes *enjoy* helping around the house."

"What's a Six?" Jannie scowled. "Am *I* a Six?"

"You're a *snicks*," Sally said, leaning forward to look around me at her sister, "an old snicks."

"And Sally is a Three and Laurie is a Nine."

"Then are you a Thirty-Four?"

"Thirty-Two."

"I will tell Laurie he is a Nine," Sally said, sliding in one movement off the couch and landing walking. Jannie and I watched her open the study door. "You are both snicks," she announced.

"—Thaler," my husband's voice said. "See if there ever *was* such a country as Thaler." He sounded a little shrill. Sally closed the door. "*I* told them," she said, coming back and climbing onto the couch.

"Mother is of course," I read, "interested in her *own* activities, such as Parent-Teachers meetings, cooking for the Girl Scouts, sewing costumes for—" I stopped. "Now what?" I inquired vaguely.

"Brownies," Jannie said. "You promised you would make brownies for the school party."

"I must have been crazy," I said. I leaned back comfortably. "My *own* activities, it says here," I said. "Taking a nap, for instance."

Jannie laughed shortly. "That is the silliest thing I ever did hear," she said. "What does it ever say in there about mommies sleeping?"

"It says I should be relaxed." I ran my finger hopefully down the lines. "It says naturally Mother is not going to handicap her children by teaching them insecure patterns of behavior; what would we think, for instance, of a mother who believed herself fond of her children, who nevertheless allowed them to see her in a temper? Or who told them obviously untruthful stories, broke promises, or showed malice?"

"You better make those brownies," Jannie said acutely. "What does show mals mean?"

"You remember?" I asked, "when you told Daddy about my running the car into a telephone pole?"

Jannie grinned. "You said I was a tattletale. You said I–"

"Yes," I said. "Well, that was foursquare, honest-to-goodness malice, right off the boat, and according to the lady who wrote this I should never have said it."

"Well, I'm not a–"

"You are *so*. And every time I think of your babbling to Daddy about that telephone pole I want to–"

"*I* didn't," Sally said. "*I* didn't tell Daddy anything. I will tell him now," and I grabbed for her too late as she slid off the couch again and went to the study door. "Go away," her father said, as she opened it.

"Mommy hit a pole," Sally said.

"*Again?*" My husband's voice rose.

"No, no, no, no, no," I said, coming after Sally. "Sally was just chattering."

"Tattletale," Jannie said promptly.

I stepped in front of her and asked gracefully, "How are the new coins coming along?"

Laurie smiled at me weakly. "So far," he said, "we have a hundred and seventy-five counterfeits."

"Oh, splendid," I said. "I thought there were only a hundred to start with. How does it happen that—"

"Will you *please* close that *door?*" my husband said.

The girls skittering ahead of me, I closed the door sharply and went through the living room and into the kitchen, where I brought up sharply before the sink and the breakfast dishes. "Well," I said brightly, "time to get to work."

"Did Daddy show mals?" Jannie asked. "Who was the lady who wrote all those things?"

"A lady who works with children," I said absent-mindedly, wondering at a sound which came from the study as of many coins crashing against the wall, and calculating with another part of my mind whether there was enough chocolate for brownies, or whether I would have to run out and get some, and hearing with still another part of my mind Jannie's wise voice saying, "Not like mommies, then. Ladies work with children, and mommies *play* with them."

"And *you*'re a snick," Sally said.

Dreamily, rinsing glasses, I had wandered on to cheerful reflections on our holiday season, which included, besides Christmas and Thanksgiving, five birthdays and an anniversary, and which seemed to be racing on with its usual neckbreaking speed, although it seemed at the same time that the days would never pass. It seemed, too, increasingly clear that our hopes for a sixth birthday in our family during the holiday season might be optimistic; the suitcase which Jannie and I share was sitting, packed, in the corner of the bedroom, contemplated lovingly by me the last thing at night and the first thing in the morning–although, as it turned out, what I was contemplating lovingly this time was a suitcase containing Jannie's yellow sundress and a jigsaw puzzle, with which she had secretly replaced my blue satin bedjacket and a dozen mystery stories and a rough draft of an informative letter beginning "Dear . . . Well, we have a new son/daughter, and so this makes two pair/three of a kind . . ." Since I did not find out, as it happened, that Jannie had repacked the suitcase until I reached the hospital, my fond regard was not in any way tarnished, although secret fears about last-minute Christmas shopping had touched the back of my mind. The same old baby clothes, much the worse for Sally's vigorous infancy, were in the bottom dresser drawer, and there was half a can of Dextro-Maltose 1 in the kitchen cabinet. "It's the home stretch again," my doctor told me affably, apparently relying upon some medical doctrine about any metaphor suiting–by now–the mother of four, "out of the trenches by Christmas." He used to laugh every time he said this.

Oddly enough, the children were able to continue their theoretically normal lives. Laurie pursued his project, for which he vaguely believed he would have a silver arrow from the Cub Scouts, of writing down all the numbers in sequence until he reached infinity; he was at this time well up into the millions, with infinity nowhere in sight. Sally was comfortably settled in nursery school, from which she brought home daily bulletins about a Mr. Grassable (who had as friends Mr. Dirtable and Mr. Sandable) and a gentleman named David who brought gum with him every morning. Jannie followed her own social life, which was only nominally affected by our family holiday season, and which required a good deal of backing and filling on my part. I became reconciled to the last-minute race to town to pick up a book or a toy or a paint set for Jannie to take to a party; invitations arrived by mail and by phone, and it was at last necessary to invest in three extra pair of white socks, to take care of Jannie's social obligations. The afternoon of Rita's party we climbed into the car, Jannie and I, at three o'clock, thanking heaven that Sally had chosen to sleep until now, and making a final check before we started. Jannie was wearing her green party dress, which she had of course chosen herself; it had a tiny white collar and rows of smocking. She had on the official white socks and her school shoes neatly shined, by me. Her best coat still fit her–although it had begun to look like Sally in another month or so–and she was wearing her green beret. She was carrying a small package with a carefully chosen doll inside; the package was wrapped in green tissue paper and the card enclosed was signed, typically, "ennaoJ." There were green bows on her pigtails, and she was wearing, as a special favor, her coral necklace. She looked very grown-up, and unbelievably pretty.

"Have you got a handkerchief?" I asked her before I started the car, and she nodded gravely, deeply aware of her green bows.

"I brought my invitation," she said. "In case we forgot the time or something."

"I only wish I knew more about the people," I said, looking at the invitation with hope, as though its pattern of pink balloons and bright lettering might somehow indicate what sort of person had paid a dime for six of them at the five and ten; "I feel a little bit worried, letting you go off to a strange house."

"I got an *invitation*," Jannie said.

I sighed, and started the car. "She sounded all *right*," I said, "the little girl's mother, I mean. When I called her to get directions to the house, she sounded all right. Richmond Road," I said, "and turn left at the private school."

"I say 'Thank you very much, Mrs. Arden,' when I'm ready to go home."

"Did you say you had a handkerchief?" We turned onto Richmond Road and Jannie settled back and folded her hands in her lap, no longer the everyday Jannie who rode with me, in her blue snow suit, to the grocery and the post office and the bakery, but a dressed-up lady in a white collar and a green beret; "Is Rita a polite little girl?" I asked with great casualness.

"She's all right," Jannie said. "From school."

I have always remembered a birthday party I went to where all the children were older, and strangers, and I sat in a corner all afternoon determined not to cry. "Do you know who else will be there?"

"Pals of mine," Jannie said, exasperated. "From *school.*"

"I suppose it's all right," I said.

"Well, now that I'm all dressed and everything," Jannie said.

I peered through the window. "Left at the private school," I said. "We watch for Overlea Drive and turn right. Then there's a sign saying Arden halfway up the hill. She said we couldn't miss it."

"Tell Sally I'll bring her some candy," Jannie said as we made a hesitant left turn around the private school, "and I'll bring Laurie some cake. And don't plan on any supper for *me* tonight–I'll be too full from the party. And the invitation says the party is over at five, so you come and get me maybe about five-thirty. That," she explained, "will give me time to pick up candy and stuff that people have forgotten about, so I can bring it to Sally."

"Have you got a handkerchief? Overlea Drive."

"And I say," Jannie went on, her tone sharpening, "I say 'Thank you, Mrs. Arden,' when I'm ready to come home. And I *have* got a handkerchief."

"Sign saying Arden," I said, "sign saying Arden."

"I've never been here before, you know," Jannie said. "Rita doesn't take the school bus."

"I'm surprised, living so far away from the school," I said. "Sign saying Arden, Private Road."

I turned the car and had to shift into second. "The chauffeur brings her," Jannie said. "I wonder if that's Rita's house way up there?"

It was the only house in sight. We were driving past terraced lawns, rich with ornamental trees and graveled walks; I saw a sundial and what may have been a swimming pool. Above us, on the top of the hill, the house looked like someone's dream of a country club, with picture windows and fieldstone and gabled roofs. "Is that where *we*'re going?" I asked, turning to look at Jannie.

"Seven chimneys," she said. "Rita always *said* she lived in a big house."

We turned onto a circled driveway which took us past a garage holding, I thought, three foreign cars, and came around to the front door. We stopped abruptly because the car parked by the front door was so soft and low and shiny that the irresistable thought of bumping it and perhaps putting a scratch on its fender (that *was* a fender?) made my teeth chatter. One of a pair of matched gray poodles rose lazily from the wide front steps and looked down at us. "Jannie," I said, "look, honey, I've only got on my blue jeans and my old jacket. And my loafers. I'll just wait here and you run on up and ring the door bell. I'll just wait here and see that you get in all right."

Jannie turned and stared at me. "Why don't you come

up to the door?" she said. "You're my mother, aren't you?"

"Yes," I said doubtfully, and climbed out after her. She ran up the steps, nodded cheerfully at the poodles when they approached her, and rang the bell; I followed gingerly, edging up the steps and moving aside briskly when one of the poodles came too close. I had a sudden rich picture of the years ahead, with me hanging around in the shrubbery trying to catch a glimpse of my beautifully-gowned daughter waltzing in the ballroom, and then the door was opened by a maid in a yellow uniform, and behind her clustered a group of little girls in party dresses pink, blue, and white.

"Hi, kids," said Jannie.

"It's *Joanne*," said a little girl in blue, who was apparently the hostess, "*now* we can start the party."

"And *this*," said Jannie grandly, "is *my* mother."

The little girl in blue curtsied, I almost curtsied back, and Jannie said, as they turned to go inside, "*We* live in a bigger house than *this*," and then called back to me, "Don't forget to tell Sally what I'm bringing her," as the door closed.

When I came back to get Jannie at five-fifteen, which I thought a neat compromise on time between the invitation and Jannie's obviously superior planning, I had put on a skirt and a pair of decent shoes. When I rang the doorbell the maid asked me inside, and I waited for barely a minute, listening to the sound of small girls' voices screaming happily from somewhere within, before a woman in gray taffeta and what were probably real emeralds—I would have believed anything by then—came to me, holding out both her hands to take mine.

"So *you*'re Joanne's mother," she said. "*Won't* you come in and have a drink?"

AT ABOUT FOUR o'clock on a Thursday afternoon the express man delivered a huge cardboard box containing a vast collection of curtains and drapes, found in an attic and sent along by my mother, in the hopes that I could use some and make the rest into slip covers or bedspreads or dusting cloths. I took the curtains out and left the big box in the front hall, meaning to take it out and leave it for the trash man when I came downstairs to make dinner. At about four-ten Laurie came out of his room, where he had been painting, and wandered into the bedroom where I was sorting the curtains out on the bed.

"What's the big box downstairs?"

"Some things came in it," I said.

"Presents?"

"No, these curtains."

"Who wants *curtains?*"

At about four-thirteen Sally woke up from her nap, and went down the stairs head first, on her stomach, bumping from step to step and calling me. When she finally found me in the bedroom, after calling me through all the rooms in the house, she asked immediately, "Is it for me?"

"Is what for you?"

"The present. Downstairs, in the hall."

"No," I said, "it was for me. These curtains."

"Can I have them?"

"No."

"*You* can't come to *my* house."

At four-thirty precisely Jannie arrived home, trotted up the front walk, opened the door, and fell over the box in the hall. "Who put this here for me to trip over?" she asked indignantly.

"Mommy's junk came in it," Laurie said. I was by now in the study, inquiring if my husband would like a cocktail before dinner. He said no, he was working on an article about a woman with second sight, and he wanted to keep his own head clear. I went into the kitchen and half-heartedly began to take potatoes out of the bag. Jannie came into the kitchen and asked if she and Laurie and Sally might play with the big box in the hall, and I said yes, if they were quiet, because Daddy was working.

Nearly ten minutes later, after a good deal of giggling and screaming and two trips outside the study by my husband, once to the hallway to say to the children that if they could not keep quiet their mother would send them all to their rooms and once to the kitchen door to say to me that he could not work on the woman with second sight so long as those children were making so much noise,

Laurie suddenly appeared in the kitchen and said delightedly, "Another present came, a real *birthday* present."

Wearily, having been half-expecting it, I put down the paring knife and followed Laurie through the study into the hall. My husband looked up as we passed and said, "This is a study, not a thoroughfare."

In the hall was the same big box, full of something which giggled and kicked around considerably. Laurie and Jannie watched pleasurably while I carefully opened the box, and when Sally popped out everyone screamed with surprise and hilarity. "I don't want *this* present," I said agreeably, "Tell the mailman to take it back." Everyone laughed again, and I went back to the kitchen.

Two minutes later Laurie reappeared in the kitchen. "*Another* present came," he announced.

Since I could not think of any good reason for persisting pig-headedly in my dinner preparations, I put down the paring knife and followed him through the study into the hall. "This is a study, not a thoroughfare," my husband said as we went through.

In the hall Sally and Laurie stood tensely while I opened the box and found Jannie. "I don't want *this* present at all," I said. "Tell the mailman to take this one along with the other." Everyone laughed.

I went back into the kitchen and in another minute Jannie and Sally came in to me. "Another present," Jannie said, and Sally added, "It's got *Laurie* in it *now*."

"This is a study, not a thoroughfare," my husband said as we all went past.

I opened the box, found Laurie, everyone laughed, and I said, "I don't want *this* present, either; tell the mailman to take them all back."

I went back into the kitchen and took up the paring knife again, feeling mildly complacent over my participation in the children's harmless games. There was a short, murmurous moment in the hall, and then the study door from the hall opened and my husband said, "This is a study, not a thoroughfare." Then a great deal of whispering went on in the study, and finally my husband said, "All right, but just once." After that there was much suppressed giggling from the hall.

I was opening the oven door when Laurie, Jannie, and Sally came into the kitchen. "*Another*–" Laurie began, and then, "What's *that?*"

"I read about it in a magazine," I said shyly. "It's got tunafish and whipped cream and potatoes and chopped olives and black bean soup and sweet pickles and all sorts of good things."

"I don't like it," said Sally at once.

"Well," Laurie said compromisingly, "what's for dessert?"

"Canned peaches," I said. "You see, I spent all afternoon with those curtains and–"

"Tunafish?" said Jannie. "Please may I have some without tunafish?"

"I believe I'll make myself a peanut butter sandwich while I'm waiting," Laurie said.

"Girls, you can start setting the table," I said. "Jannie, cups and glasses. Sally, table mats and silver."

"*I* want to do glasses," Sally said at once.

"Don't forget the salt and pepper. Casserole, bread, salad, peaches." I scowled indecisively at the oven door. "What would happen," I asked Jannie, "if I put in tomato sauce?"

"It would be even worse," Jannie said cheerfully.

"Clean towels," I said. "I'll be right down; Laurie, you wash your hands before you touch that bread."

I went out of the kitchen and through the study and through the hall and up the stairs, found the clean towels and brought them down again. "Supper in about five minutes," I said as I went through the study; "Supper in about five minutes," I said as I went past the dining room, "Supper in about five minutes," I said as I came into the kitchen. "Laurie, start telling Dad supper is ready."

Laurie went into the study and came back. "Not there," he said.

"He probably went to wash," Jannie said.

"Salt and pepper," I said, surveying the table. Jannie had set everything left-handed, as usual.

"*I* washed," Sally said, coming out of the bathroom. I glanced beyond her to the clean towel I had just hung on the rack, and sighed. "Laurie and Jannie, wash," I said. "Dad ought to be down in a minute."

"Seems like there was something I meant to tell you," Laurie said, taking his place at the table with his peanut butter sandwich.

"You call those hands clean?"

"I said I didn't *like* this," Jannie said, looking into her plate.

"Seems like it was something about Dad," Laurie said.

NINKI HAD FOUR black and white kittens on December fifth. Their eyes opened, they began to tumble delightfully together on the kitchen floor, and Ninki, svelte and lively, got back to her mouse-hunting. I continued to come downstairs each morning step by step, holding on to the bannister. The morning the first snow fell I came into the kitchen where Jannie and Sally were eating oatmeal at the yellow table, and Elsie, a nice girl whom I had hired to stay with us until the first of the year, was cheerfully spreading mustard on Laurie's lunch sandwiches.

"Good morning," Elsie said brightly. "Still with us, I see?"

"Yeah," I said. "Coffee?"

"Good morning, Mommy dear," said Jannie, in the sweet voice which means she has decided to hold out on her oatmeal until ten minutes to nine, and Sally echoed, "Good morning, Mommy dear, dear morning, good Mommy."

"Uh," I said.

"Thought I heard the car go out last night," Elsie said conversationally, "but then I thought you'd surely wake me if you were going."

"I surely would," I said.

"And how do you feel? Well?"

"I surely do," I said. I took my coffee into the dining room and settled down with the morning paper. A woman in New York had had twins in a taxi. A woman in Ohio had just had her seventeenth child. A twelve-year-old girl in Mexico had given birth to a thirteen-pound boy. The lead article on the woman's page was about how to adjust the older child to the new baby. I finally found an account of an axe murder on page seventeen, and held my coffee cup up to my face to see if the steam might revive me.

"Laurie," Elsie said at the back stairs, "ten minutes after eight."

"I'm *coming*," Laurie said. "Mommy still here?"

"She surely is," Elsie said gaily. "Brush your teeth."

I turned to the sports page.

Jannie's voice rose clearly from the kitchen. "When we get our baby brother," she asked, "will he have his breakfast out here with us?"

"Oatmeal?" Sally added.

"He'll be very tiny," Elsie told them, "and at first he'll spend all his time in the crib and he'll have all his meals from a bottle."

"And I'm going to give him a bath," Jannie said.

"And I'm going to give him some of my oatmeal," Sally said.

"Let's ask Mommy when he's coming," Jannie said.

"Never you mind," Elsie said hastily "Finish that oatmeal."

Laurie came crashing downstairs and I heard my husband's feet hit the floor beside the bed. "Good morning, Mommy," Laurie called from the kitchen. "I was sure you'd be gone *today*."

"Yeah."

Laurie brought his tray in and set it on the table; he began to spoon sugar thoughtfully onto his oatmeal. "You know," he said, "you don't suppose you won't go at all, do you?"

"I've thought of it," I said.

Laurie began to laugh uproariously. "All those baby clothes," he said.

"That's enough sugar," I said. "Read the paper or something."

Laurie took the sports section and propped it up against the coffee pot. "By the way," he said suddenly, looking up from the paper, "the teacher asked me yesterday again what about my baby brother. She's going to sing 'Happy Birthday to You' when it comes."

"Tell her I've gone to Mexico," I said.

My husband came downstairs at that moment, glanced

at me with some surprise, and said, "Good morning, good morning."

"Good morning, Dad," Laurie said. "Mommy's still here."

"Good morning," my husband said in the kitchen to Elsie and the girls, and I could hear Elsie telling him that she had surely thought we would wake her if we left during the night.

My husband brought his tray in and set it down on the table.

"Coins from Hong-Kong should be here today," Laurie told him.

"Ought to write that fellow," my husband said vaguely.

"How do you figure about Mommy?" Laurie asked.

My husband looked searchingly at me. "Damned if *I* know," he said.

I lifted my head from the steam of my coffee. "Look," I said bitterly, "I could go stay in a hotel somewhere and write you when it's all over."

"How do you feel?" my husband asked.

"Bah," I said distinctly.

"So long as you don't have any *children* today," Laurie said. "You got to pick me up at Cub Scouts at five."

"Tomorrow?"

"No," said my husband. "Tomorrow is the Numismatic Society and I didn't go the last time because I had a cold and I didn't go the time before because your mother was here and I'd hate to miss it *again* for a trifle."

"And Sunday of course your aunt and uncle are coming," I told my husband. "How about Monday?"

Elsie put her head around the corner of the kitchen door. "Monday morning I take my driving test," she said, "so don't go before Monday afternoon. I can drive you. And then of course on Tuesday Jannie goes to Kathy's party."

"Wednesday?"

"I *was* planning to visit my sister," Elsie said. "You remember you said it would be all right, you said you would probably be back from the hospital by then and–"

"Is Thursday fairly clear for everybody?" I asked, my voice rising.

"Well, *Friday*," Laurie said, worried, "Friday is Cub Scouts again."

"Have the baby on my birthday," Jannie called from the kitchen.

Jannie's birthday was ten months and some days off. "I'll try to make it," I said.

Laurie laughed. "Mr. Feeley says if the baby's born before Tuesday he'll give you ten percent of his winnings."

"What winnings?" I asked.

Laurie glanced, dismayed, at his father, and his father said elaborately, rising from his chair, "Want to take another look at those Roman coins, son?"

"*What* winnings?" I said insistently.

"Nothing to worry about," my husband said. "Just

something we were . . ." He thought. "Making for the baby," he finished finally.

"A book," Laurie added helpfully.

His father glanced at him with respect. "That's right," he said, "a baby book."

They headed for the study. "It *couldn't* be before Tuesday," my husband was saying to Laurie, as one continuing a private discussion, "the law of probability . . ."

"Ross told me in school yesterday he wants a dime on Christmas Day," Laurie said.

"Tell him we'll give him thirty to one," my husband said.

From the study I could hear my husband saying that Ross's money was as good as gone, and Laurie remarked that he thought he could count the teacher in for maybe even a quarter.

"I wouldn't like to see any more money go on Tuesday," my husband remarked absently, "you can't count on *her* to figure the odds, you know."

"Just like her to pick a day with no money in it," Laurie confirmed. "Is this Nero, Dad?"

"It's the button from my jacket," my husband said. "I meant to ask Jannie to sew it on."

I lighted another cigarette and poured hot coffee into my cup; it did not seem worthwhile doing anything else. "Ten minutes of nine," Elsie remarked in the kitchen.

With a great shout Sally slid off her chair and Jannie

followed. "Come back here and finish this oatmeal," Elsie said as they raced for the front door.

"Bye, Dad," Laurie said. He went through the kitchen to get his lunch box, and stopped in the dining room on his way to the front door. "See you at five?" he asked me.

"Oh, surely, surely," I said.

I followed them to the front door and waved as they got into the school bus; Sally sat at the front window to watch for the station wagon which would take her to nursery school. The mail had come, and I got Sally to pick it up off the floor for me and then went with it into the study.

"All bills today," I said maliciously to my husband.

"Again?" he said. "It seems like it was only—"

"Pay them in Roman coins," I said. I sat down in the straight chair I had brought into the study especially; the upholstered chairs are difficult to get out of without a struggle. "Pay them with your eleven Siamese gambling house tokens," I said.

My husband glanced at me apprehensively. "How do you feel?"

"Pay them in counterfeit Scottish merks," I said. "I feel fine."

My husband touched the stack of mail with one finger, timidly. "One of us," he said, "has got to go to the bank and see Mr. Andrews."

"Not me," I said.

"Of course not," my husband said soothingly. "You

can go in tomorrow morning," he added, "if you're still here."

Our local bank is an informal and neighborly spot, lavish with its hard-covered checkbooks, always ready to look up the value of the Swiss franc, eager to advise on investments or make wills. Its atmosphere is substantially less hushed and reverent than, say, a good movie theatre, with a loud-speaker system which plays soft music for depositors, an air-cooling device which clears the air of the acrid scent of ten-dollar bills, richly upholstered benches for nervous mortgagees; it is a bank dedicated to every friendly pursuit except the swift transference of money. I have had occasion, over the past few years, to deal frequently with the bank's Mr. Andrews, a man of chilling questions and a very cynical view of me, over some minor monies which have passed reluctantly from Mr. Andrews' hands into our bank account, and rapidly from there into the hands of various milkmen, doctors, department stores, and sundry poker cronies of my husband's. Mr. Andrews likes to believe that he is giving me this money as a favor. "We are always glad to lend funds," he is apt to say, with a dim smile, "after all, that's what a bank is *for*, isn't it?" Since Mr. Andrews so obviously believes that that is the main thing that a bank is *not* for, my answer to this is usually a gay laugh and a quick question about how ninety days is six months, isn't it? Mr. Andrews is also fond of saying things like, "Well, *we* have our obligations to meet, too, you realize," and "If we were to accommodate *every*one who asks us . . ."

Mr. Andrews never says "money," just like that, the way the rest of us do so often; he refers to it reverently as "Credit" or "Funds" or "Equity." I have fallen into the habit of taking one or more of my children with me when I drop in to speak to Mr. Andrews about equity or funds or credit, in the unexpressed hope that their soft pathetic eyes might touch Mr. Andrews' heart, although I know by now that their soft pathetic little eyes might as easily open the door to the vault; the only time, I think, that I have ever seen Mr. Andrews really taken aback was when Laurie, when he had just commenced coin-collecting, asked if he might look over the bank's small change for V nickels.

At any rate, shortly before Christmas, then—and Christmas is of course always a time of great monetary discomfort around our house—I came timidly to Mr. Andrews' bank, at the back of my mind the thought that the children's presents had at least been bought and duly hidden, although not paid for, and holding by one hand my daughter Jannie, in a blue snow suit, and holding by the other hand my daughter Sally, in a red snow suit. The girls had their hair brushed and their boots on the right feet, and if I could raise the cash from Mr. Andrews they were each going to have an ice cream cone. We came into the bank, where the loudspeaker system was playing "Joy to the World," and found that the center paddock, where they usually foreclose mortgages, had been given over to a tall and gracious Christmas tree; because of the holiday season, they were foreclosing their mortgages in a sort of little recess behind the tellers. I sat the girls down on a velvet-covered bench directly in front of the Christmas tree, and told them to stay right where they were and Mommy would be back in a minute and then we would all go and get our ice cream cones. They sat down obediently, and I made my way over to Mr. Andrews' secretary.

"Good morning," I said to her.

"Good morning," she said. "Merry Christmas."

"Oh," I said. "Merry Christmas."

She nodded brightly and turned back to the papers on her desk. I twined my fingers around the ornamental iron-work of the railing, and said, "I wonder if I might perhaps be able to see Mr. Andrews?"

"Mr. Andrews? And what did you want to see him about?"

"Well," I said, coming a little closer, "it was to have been about our loan."

"Your loan?" she said, in that peculiarly penetrating tone all bank employees use when there is a question of money going the unnatural, or reverse-English direction. "You wanted to pay back your loan?"

"I hoped," I said, "that perhaps I could speak to Mr. Andrews."

"Isn't that sweet?" she said unexpectedly.

After a minute I realized that she was staring past me to where my girls were sitting, and I turned and saw without belief that Santa Claus, complete with sack of toys, had come out from behind the Christmas tree and was leaning over the railing and beckoning my daughters to him.

"I didn't know the bank had a Santa Claus," I said.

"Every year," she said. "At Christmas, you know."

Jannie and Sally slid off the bench and trotted over to Santa Claus; I could hear Sally's delighted, "Hello, Santa Claus!" and see Jannie's half-embarrassed smile; people all over the bank were turning to look and to beam and to smile at one another and murmur appreciatively. Because I have known Jannie and Sally for rather a long time, I untwined my fingers from the ironwork and made across the bank for their bench, reaching them just as Santa Claus opened the little gate in the railing and ushered them inside. He sat down under the warm lights of the Christmas tree and took Jannie onto one knee and Sally onto the other.

"Well, well, well," he said, and laughed hugely. "And have you been a *good* girl?" he asked Jannie.

Jannie nodded, her mouth open, and Sally said, "I've been *very* good."

"And do you brush your teeth?"

"Twice," said Sally, and Jannie said, "*I* brush *my* teeth every morning and every night and every morning."

"Well, well, well," Santa Claus said, nodding his head appreciatively. "So you've been good little girls, have you?"

"I've been very *very* good," Sally said insistently.

Santa Claus thought. "And have you washed your faces?" was what he finally achieved.

"I wash *my* face," said Sally, and Jannie, inspired, said, "I wash my face and my hands and my arms and my ears and my neck and—"

"Well, that's just *fine*," Santa Claus said, and again he laughed merrily, caroming Jannie and Sally off his round little belly. "Fine, fine," he said, "and now," he said to Jannie, "what is old Santa going to bring you for Christmas?"

"A doll?" Jannie said tentatively, "are you going to bring me a doll?"

"I most certainly *am* going to bring you a doll," said Santa Claus. "I'm going to bring you the prettiest doll you ever *saw*, because you've been such a *good* girl."

"And a wagon?" Jannie said, "and doll dishes and a little stove?"

"That's *just* what I'm going to bring you," Santa Claus said. "I'm going to bring good little girls *every*thing they ask for."

The fatuous smile I had been wearing on my face began to slip a little; there was a handsome doll dressed in blue waiting for Jannie in the guest room closet, and a handsome doll dressed in pink waiting for Sally; I began trying to signal surreptitiously to Santa Claus.

"And me," Sally said, "and me, and *me*, I want a bicycle."

I shook my head most violently at Santa Claus, smiling nervously. "That's right," Santa Claus said, "for good little girls, I bring bicycles."

"You're *really* going to bring me a bicycle?" Sally asked incredulously, "*and* a doll *and* a wagon?"

"I most certainly am," Santa Claus told her.

Sally gazed raptly at Jannie. "He's going to bring my bicycle after all," she said.

"*I* want a bicycle too," Jannie said.

"Alllllll right," said Santa Claus. "But have you been a *good* girl?" he asked Jannie anxiously.

"I've been so good," Jannie told him with ardor, "you just don't *know*, I've been so good."

"I've been good," Sally said. "I want blocks, too. And a doll carriage for my doll, and a bicycle."

"And our brother wants a microscope," Jannie told Santa Claus, "and he's been a very good boy. And a little table and chairs, I want."

"Santa Claus," I said, "*excuse* me, Santa Claus. . . ."

"Aren't they darling?" a woman said behind me.

"And candy, and oranges, and nuts," Santa Claus was going on blissfully, "and all sorts of good things in your stockings, and candy canes—"

"I forgot, I want a party dress."

"But you must be *good* little girls, and do just what your mommy and daddy tell you to, and never *never* forget to brush your teeth."

I went with haste back to Mr. Andrews' secretary. "I've *got* to see Mr. Andrews," I told her, "I've got to see him *fast*."

"You'll have to wait," she said, looking fondly over to where my daughters were receiving a final pat on the head from Santa Claus.

The loudspeaker system was playing "O Come, All Ye Faithful," I was thinking wildly: bicycle, microscope, bicycle, table and chairs, doll dishes, and my daughters came running across the floor to me. "Look," Sally was shrieking, "look at what Santa Claus gave to us."

"Santa Claus was here," Jannie confirmed, "he came right into the bank where we were and he gave us each a present, look, a little bag of chocolate money."

"Oh, fine, fine, fine," I said madly.

"And I *am* going to have my bicycle, Santa said he was *too* bringing it."

"—and me a bicycle too, and doll carriages and dishes and—"

"—and in our stockings."

"Mr. Andrews will see you now," said the secretary.

I sat my daughters down again and made my entrance into Mr. Andrews' office. His nose still retained a trace of jovial redness, but the jolly old elf's eye was the familiar agate, and the faint echo of jingle bells around him sounded more like the clinking of half dollars.

"Well," said Santa Claus, selecting my loan slip from the stack on his desk, "and what brings *you* here again so soon?'

IT WAS A beautiful morning, cold and clear and full of color, and the taxi driver was just finishing a story about how his wife's mother had come to visit them and canned all the peaches his wife had been planning to put into their freezer. "Just wasted the whole lot of them," he said, and pulled up in front of the house with a flourish.

"There are the children on the porch," I said.

"Beginning to seem like Christmas," my husband said to the taxi driver as I got out, and the taxi driver said, "Snow before morning."

Jannie's hair had obviously not been combed since I left, and as I went up the front walk I was resolving to make her tell immediately where she had hidden the hairbrush. She was wearing her dearest summer sundress, and she was barefoot. Laurie needed a haircut, and he had on his old sneakers, one of which no longer laces, but fastens with a safety pin; I had made a particular point of throwing those sneakers into the garbage can before I left. Sally had chocolate all over her face and *she* was wearing Laurie's fur hat. All three of them were leaning over the porch rail, still and expectant.

I tried to catch hold of all three of them at once, but they evaded me skillfully and ran at their father. "Did you bring it?" Jannie demanded, "did you bring it, did you bring it, did you bring it?"

"Is *that* it you're carrying?" Laurie demanded sternly, "that *little* thing?"

"Did you *bring* it?" Jannie insisted.

"Come indoors and I'll show you," their father said.

They followed him into the living room, and stood in a solemn row by the couch. "Now don't touch," their father said, and they nodded all together. They watched while he carefully set the bundle down on the couch and unwrapped it.

Then, into the stunned silence which followed, Sally finally said, "What is it?"

"It's a baby," said their father, with an edge of nervousness to his voice, "it's a baby boy and its name is Barry."

"What's a baby?" Sally asked me.

"It's pretty small," Laurie said doubtfully. "Is that the best you could get?"

"I tried to get another, a bigger one," I said with irritation, "but the doctor said this was the only one left."

"My goodness," said Jannie, "what are we going to do with *that?* Anyway," she said, "*you*'re back."

Suddenly she and Sally were both climbing onto my lap at once, and Laurie came closer and allowed me to kiss him swiftly on the cheek; I discovered that I could reach around all three of them, something I had not been able to do for some time.

"Well," Laurie said, anxious to terminate this sentimental scene, "so now we've got this baby. Do you think it will grow?" he asked his father.

"It's got very small feet," Jannie said. "I really believe they're *too* small."

"Well, if you don't like it we can *always* take it back," said their father.

"Oh, we like it all right, I guess," Laurie said comfortingly. "It's only that I guess we figured on something a little bigger."

"What *is* it?" asked Sally, unconvinced. She put out a tentative finger and touched one toe. "Is this its foot?"

"Please start calling it 'him,' " I said.

"Him?" said Sally. "Him?"

"Hi, Barry," said Laurie, leaning down to look directly into one open blue eye, "hi, Barry, hi, Barry, hi, Barry."

"Hi, Barry," said Jannie.

"Hi, Barry," said Sally. "Is this your foot?"

"I suppose it'll cry a lot?" Laurie asked his father, man to man.

His father shrugged. "Not much else it *can* do," he pointed out.

"I remember Jannie cried all the time," Laurie went on.

"I did not," Jannie said. "*You* were the one cried all the time."

"Did you get it at the hospital?" Sally asked. She moved Barry's foot up and down and he curled his toes.

"Yes," I said.

"Why didn't you take me?" Sally asked.

"I took you the last time," I said.

"What did you say its name was?" Sally asked.

"Barry," I said.

"Barry?"

"Barry."

"Where did you get it?"

"Well," Laurie said. He sighed and stretched. "Better take a look at those Greek tetradrachms," he said.

"Right," said his father, rising.

"Jannie, you go find that hairbrush," I said.

Laurie, on his way out of the room, stopped next to me and hesitated, obviously trying to think of something congratulatory to say. "I guess it *will* be nice for you, though," he said at last. "Something to keep you busy now *we*'re all grown up."

APPENDIX: HANDBILL

SOME POLTERGEIST INCIDENTS IN THE RESIDENCE OF S.E.H., ESQUIRE

With a Moſt Intereſting Diſcuſſion of the Probable Reſults of ſuch Diſturbances in the Dwelling of a Gentleman.

Mr. H. depoſing, That, Having lived upon this houſe for more than ſeven years together, he has until recent months ſeen no evidence of ſupernatural poſſeſſion, Until, within the months just paſt, when his houſe has become ſeemingly a meeting-place, or neſt, for demonic ſpirits;

That, for the ſpace of more than three nights together, his ſamily has been diſturbed by the ſounds of a great running, or ſtamping, which, going on above half an Hour at a time, has cauſed the greateſt Apprehenſion among them;

That his Wife, a Female of nervous diſpoſition and eaſily excited, almost into Frenzies by Supernatural Manifeſtations, has at ſeveral ſeparate times been troubled by the Night Mares, as of a Perſonage whiſpering into her Ear ſecrets of Horror;

That, having as was her cuſtom the daily ſpoons in her hand and ſetting them one by one into the Beauſet, ſhe has had at different times one ſpoon or another taken ſorcibly ſrom her hand and on one ocaſion this ſpoon was aſter-ward hurled, or thrown, violently at her Head;

That, ſince theſe maniſeſtations, a cabinet door belonging to a Televiſion ſet, will neither ſtay cloſed nor ſuſſer itſelſ to be latched, although ſour ſeparate Carpenters en-deavored to perſuade it ſhut with their Hammars and a Mr. Feeley, a gentleman, being newly come into the houſe, did ſtrike it moſt violently with his ſoot;

That Miſter H.'s ſon, a child of ſome eight or ten years, doth ſo conſtruct nightly with his leſſon-books a Barrier, or Wall, againſt the doorway of his nurſery, in order, as he ſays, to *keep out the goblins*, and he doth, beſides this, ſay that he hath ſeen ſeveral times a Wolſ, or other large black animal, upon the Rooſ outſide his Window;

That at night recently, this Maniſeſtation did take up a Kniſe, or Dirque, which Miſter H. doth always keep by him leſt ſootpads come upon him ſuddenly and unawares, and daſh'd it ſo wildly againſt the wall that it like to have broke into a thouſand pieces;

That ſor the ſpace of ſome ſeven nights running, there hath been in this houſe the ſound of drums, of laughing, of ſtomping, and craſhing of objects, not to be accounted ſor even by the ſeveral children of Miſter H., and more, perhaps ſaith Mr. H., than could even be perſormed by his children without gueſts or other children in company;

Theſe things, atteſted to by Mr. H. and his ſamily, have been ſeen and witneſſed by many other perſons who have viſited Mr. H.'s houſe to obſerve them, and by the aſoreſaid Feeley, gentleman, and all ſuch perſons agree that the houſe is poſſeſſed by a Poltergeiſt, or Evil Spirit, which has in its Intent the moſt Malicious Amuſement at the expenſe of thoſe dwellers in the Houſe;

That Miſter H.'s Landlord, a man of ſome means, refuſes either to have the houſe Exorciſed or to allow Miſter H. to Looſe his Leaſe, and that thereſore Miſter H.'s only Recourſe, as he ſays, is to open his Houſe to Viſitors at a Penny a View, ſince, as he ſays, it is already become ſo ſull of Company at beſt that he may as well Charge.

7th. – 30th Jan 6th

Bus Thunderbird

J

8
~~78~~

Claremont. AARP.